W9-AXP-662

Kubernetes: Up and Running

Dive into the Future of Infrastructure

Kelsey Hightower, Brendan Burns, and Joe Beda

Beijing · Boston · Farnham · Sebastopol · Tokyo

Kubernetes: Up and Running

by Kelsey Hightower, Brendan Burns, and Joe Beda

Copyright © 2017 Kelsey Hightower, Brendan Burns, and Joe Beda. All rights reserved.

Printed in the United States of America.

Published by O'Reilly Media, Inc., 1005 Gravenstein Highway North, Sebastopol, CA 95472.

O'Reilly books may be purchased for educational, business, or sales promotional use. Online editions are also available for most titles (*http://oreilly.com/safari*). For more information, contact our corporate/institutional sales department: 800-998-9938 or *corporate@oreilly.com*.

Editor: Angela Rufino	**Indexer:** Kevin Broccoli
Production Editor: Melanie Yarbrough	**Interior Designer:** David Futato
Copyeditor: Christina Edwards	**Cover Designer:** Karen Montgomery
Proofreader: Rachel Head	**Illustrator:** Rebecca Demarest

September 2017:   First Edition

Revision History for the First Edition

2017-09-05:   First Release

See *http://oreilly.com/catalog/errata.csp?isbn=9781491935675* for release details.

The O'Reilly logo is a registered trademark of O'Reilly Media, Inc. *Kubernetes: Up and Running*, the cover image, and related trade dress are trademarks of O'Reilly Media, Inc.

While the publisher and the authors have used good faith efforts to ensure that the information and instructions contained in this work are accurate, the publisher and the authors disclaim all responsibility for errors or omissions, including without limitation responsibility for damages resulting from the use of or reliance on this work. Use of the information and instructions contained in this work is at your own risk. If any code samples or other technology this work contains or describes is subject to open source licenses or the intellectual property rights of others, it is your responsibility to ensure that your use thereof complies with such licenses and/or rights.

978-1-491-93567-5

[LSI]

For Klarissa and Kelis, who keep me sane. And for my Mom, who taught me a strong work ethic and how to rise above all odds. —Kelsey Hightower

For my Dad, who helped me fall in love with computers by bringing home punch cards and dot matrix banners. —Joe Beda

For Robin, Julia, Ethan, and everyone who bought cookies to pay for that Commodore 64 in my third-grade class. —Brendan Burns

Table of Contents

Preface

Kubernetes: A Dedication

Kubernetes would like to thank every sysadmin who has woken up at 3 a.m. to restart a process. Every developer who pushed code to production only to find that it didn't run like it did on their laptop. Every systems architect who mistakenly pointed a load test at the production service because of a leftover hostname that they hadn't updated. It was the pain, the weird hours, and the weird errors that inspired the development of Kubernetes. In a single sentence: Kubernetes intends to radically simplify the task of building, deploying, and maintaining distributed systems. It has been inspired by decades of real-world experience building reliable systems and it has been designed from the ground up to make that experience, if not euphoric, at least pleasant. We hope you enjoy the book!

Who Should Read This Book

Whether you are new to distributed systems or have been deploying cloud-native systems for years, containers and Kubernetes can help you achieve new levels of velocity, agility, reliability, and efficiency. This book describes the Kubernetes cluster orchestrator and how its tools and APIs can be used to improve the development, delivery, and maintenance of distributed applications. Though no previous experience with Kubernetes is assumed, to make maximal use of the book you should be comfortable building and deploying server-based applications. Familiarity with concepts like load balancers and network storage will be useful, though not required. Likewise, experience with Linux, Linux containers, and Docker, though not essential, will help you make the most of this book.

Why We Wrote This Book

We have been involved with Kubernetes since its very beginnings. It has been truly remarkable to watch it transform from a curiosity largely used in experiments to a crucial production-grade infrastructure that powers large-scale production applications in varied fields, from machine learning to online services. As this transition occurred, it became increasingly clear that a book that captured both how to use the core concepts in Kubernetes and the motivations behind the development of those concepts would be an important contribution to the state of cloud-native application development. We hope that in reading this book, you not only learn how to build reliable, scalable applications on top of Kubernetes, but also that you receive insight into the core challenges of distributed systems that led to its development.

A Word on Cloud-Native Applications Today

From the first programming languages, to object-oriented programming, to the development of virtualization and cloud infrastructure, the history of computer science is a history of the development of abstractions that hide complexity and empower you to build ever more sophisticated applications. Despite this, the development of reliable, scalable applications is still dramatically more challenging than it ought to be. In recent years, containers and container orchestration APIs like Kubernetes have become an important abstraction that radically simplifies the development of reliable, scalable distributed systems. Though containers and orchestrators are still in the process of entering the mainstream, they are already enabling developers to build and deploy applications with a speed, agility, and reliability that would have seemed like science fiction only a few years ago.

Navigating This Book

This book is organized as follows. The first chapter outlines the high-level benefits of Kubernetes without diving too deeply into the details. If you are new to Kubernetes, this is a great place to start to understand why you should read the rest of the book.

The following chapter provides a detailed introduction to containers and containerized application development. If you've never really played around with Docker before, this chapter will be a useful introduction. If you are already a Docker expert, it will likely be mostly review.

Chapter 3 covers how to deploy Kubernetes. While most of this book focuses on how to *use* Kubernetes, you need to get a cluster up and running before you start using it. While running a cluster for production is out of the scope of this book, this chapter presents a couple of easy ways to create a cluster so that you can understand how to use Kubernetes.

Starting with Chapter 5, we dive into the details of deploying an application using Kubernetes. We cover Pods (Chapter 5), labels and annotations (Chapter 6), services (Chapter 7), and ReplicaSets (Chapter 8). These form the core basics of what you need to deploy your service in Kubernetes.

After those chapters, we cover some more specialized objects in Kubernetes: `Daemon Sets` (Chapter 9), jobs (Chapter 10), and `ConfigMaps` and secrets (Chapter 11). While these chapters are essential for many production applications, if you are just learning Kubernetes they can be skipped and returned to later, after you gain more experience and expertise.

We then cover deployments (Chapter 12), which tie together the lifecycle of a complete application, and integrating storage into Kubernetes (Chapter 13). Finally, we conclude with some examples of how to develop and deploy real-world applications in Kubernetes.

Online Resources

You will want to install Docker (*https://docker.com*). You likely will also want to familiarize yourself with the Docker documentation if you have not already done so.

Likewise, you will want to install the `kubectl` command-line tool (*https://kubernetes.io*). You may also want to join the Kubernetes slack channel (*http://slack.kubernetes.io*), where you will find a large community of users who are willing to talk and answer questions at nearly any hour of the day.

Finally, as you grow more advanced, you may want to engage with the open source Kubernetes repository on GitHub (*https://github.com/kubernetes/kubernetes*).

Conventions Used in This Book

The following typographical conventions are used in this book:

Italic
> Indicates new terms, URLs, email addresses, filenames, and file extensions.

`Constant width`
> Used for program listings, as well as within paragraphs to refer to program elements such as variable or function names, databases, data types, environment variables, statements, and keywords.

`Constant width bold`
> Shows commands or other text that should be typed literally by the user.

`Constant width italic`
> Shows text that should be replaced with user-supplied values or by values determined by context.

This icon signifies a tip, suggestion, or general note.

This icon indicates a warning or caution.

Using Code Examples

Supplemental material (code examples, exercises, etc.) is available for download at *https://github.com/kubernetes-up-and-running/examples*.

This book is here to help you get your job done. In general, if example code is offered with this book, you may use it in your programs and documentation. You do not need to contact us for permission unless you're reproducing a significant portion of the code. For example, writing a program that uses several chunks of code from this book does not require permission. Selling or distributing a CD-ROM of examples from O'Reilly books does require permission. Answering a question by citing this book and quoting example code does not require permission. Incorporating a significant amount of example code from this book into your product's documentation does require permission.

We appreciate, but do not require, attribution. An attribution usually includes the title, author, publisher, and ISBN. For example: "*Kubernetes: Up and Running* by Kelsey Hightower, Brendan Burns, and Joe Beda (O'Reilly). Copyright 2017 Kelsey Hightower, Brendan Burns, and Joe Beda, 978-1-491-93567-5."

If you feel your use of code examples falls outside fair use or the permission given above, feel free to contact us at *permissions@oreilly.com*.

O'Reilly Safari

Safari (formerly Safari Books Online) is a membership-based training and reference platform for enterprise, government, educators, and individuals.

Members have access to thousands of books, training videos, Learning Paths, interactive tutorials, and curated playlists from over 250 publishers, including O'Reilly Media, Harvard Business Review, Prentice Hall Professional, Addison-Wesley Professional, Microsoft Press, Sams, Que, Peachpit Press, Adobe, Focal Press, Cisco Press,

John Wiley & Sons, Syngress, Morgan Kaufmann, IBM Redbooks, Packt, Adobe Press, FT Press, Apress, Manning, New Riders, McGraw-Hill, Jones & Bartlett, and Course Technology, among others.

For more information, please visit *http://oreilly.com/safari*.

How to Contact Us

Please address comments and questions concerning this book to the publisher:

O'Reilly Media, Inc.
1005 Gravenstein Highway North
Sebastopol, CA 95472
800-998-9938 (in the United States or Canada)
707-829-0515 (international or local)
707-829-0104 (fax)

We have a web page for this book, where we list errata, examples, and any additional information. You can access this page at *http://bit.ly/kubernetes-up-and-running*.

To comment or ask technical questions about this book, send email to *bookquestions@oreilly.com*.

For more information about our books, courses, conferences, and news, see our website at *http://www.oreilly.com*.

Find us on Facebook: *http://facebook.com/oreilly*

Follow us on Twitter: *http://twitter.com/oreillymedia*

Watch us on YouTube: *http://www.youtube.com/oreillymedia*

CHAPTER 1
Introduction

Kubernetes is an open source orchestrator for deploying containerized applications. Kubernetes was originally developed by Google, inspired by a decade of experience deploying scalable, reliable systems in containers via application-oriented APIs.[1]

But Kubernetes is much more than simply exporting technology developed at Google. Kubernetes has grown to be the product of a rich and growing open source community. This means that Kubernetes is a product that is suited not just to the needs of internet-scale companies but to cloud-native developers of all scales, from a cluster of Raspberry Pi computers to a warehouse full of the latest machines. Kubernetes provides the software necessary to successfully build and deploy reliable, scalable distributed systems.

You may be wondering what we mean when we say "reliable, scalable distributed systems." More and more services are delivered over the network via APIs. These APIs are often delivered by a *distributed system*, the various pieces that implement the API running on different machines, connected via the network and coordinating their actions via network communication. Because we rely on these APIs increasingly for all aspects of our daily lives (e.g., finding directions to the nearest hospital), these systems must be highly *reliable*. They cannot fail, even if a part of the system crashes or otherwise fails. Likewise, they must maintain *availability* even during software rollouts or other maintenance events. Finally, because more and more of the world is coming online and using such services, they must be highly *scalable* so that they can grow their capacity to keep up with ever-increasing usage without radical redesign of the distributed system that implements the services.

---

1 Brendan Burns et al., "Borg, Omega, and Kubernetes: Lessons Learned from Three Container-Management Systems over a Decade," *ACM Queue* 14 (2016): 70–93, available at *http://bit.ly/2vIrL4S*.

Depending on when and why you have come to hold this book in your hands, you may have varying degrees of experience with containers, distributed systems, and Kubernetes. Regardless of what your experience is, we believe this book will enable you to make the most of your use of Kubernetes.

There are many reasons why people come to use containers and container APIs like Kubernetes, but we believe they effectively all can be traced back to one of these benefits:

- Velocity
- Scaling (of both software and teams)
- Abstracting your infrastructure
- Efficiency

In the following sections we describe how Kubernetes can help provide each of these benefits.

Velocity

Velocity is the key component in nearly all software development today. The changing nature of software from boxed software shipped on CDs to web-based services that change every few hours means that the difference between you and your competitors is often the speed with which you can develop and deploy new components and features.

It is important to note, however, that this velocity is not defined in terms of simply raw speed. While your users are always looking for iterative improvement, they are more interested in a highly reliable service. Once upon a time, it was OK for a service to be down for maintenance at midnight every night. But today, our users expect constant uptime, even if the software they are running is changing constantly.

Consequently, velocity is measured not in terms of the raw number of features you can ship per hour or day, but rather in terms of the number of things you can ship while maintaining a highly available service.

In this way, containers and Kubernetes can provide the tools that you need to move quickly, while staying available. The core concepts that enable this are immutability, declarative configuration, and online self-healing systems. These ideas all interrelate to radically improve the speed with which you can reliably deploy software.

The Value of Immutability

Containers and Kubernetes encourage developers to build distributed systems that adhere to the principles of immutable infrastructure. With immutable infrastructure, once an artifact is created in the system it does not change via user modifications.

Traditionally, computers and software systems have been treated as *mutable* infrastructure. With mutable infrastructure, changes are applied as incremental updates to an existing system. A system upgrade via the `apt-get update` tool is a good example of an update to a mutable system. Running `apt` sequentially downloads any updated binaries, copies them on top of older binaries, and makes incremental updates to configuration files. With a mutable system, the current state of the infrastructure is not represented as a single artifact, but rather an accumulation of incremental updates and changes. On many systems these incremental updates come from not just system upgrades but operator modifications as well.

In contrast, in an immutable system, rather than a series of incremental updates and changes, an entirely new, complete image is built, where the update simply replaces the entire image with the newer image in a single operation. There are no incremental changes. As you can imagine, this is a significant shift from the more traditional world of configuration management.

To make this more concrete in the world of containers, consider two different ways to upgrade your software:

1. You can log into a container, run a command to download your new software, kill the old server, and start the new one.

2. You can build a new container image, push it to a container registry, kill the existing container, and start a new one.

At first blush, these two approaches might seem largely indistinguishable. So what is it about the act of building a new container that improves reliability?

The key differentiation is the artifact that you create, and the record of how you created it. These records make it easy to understand exactly the differences in some new version and, if something goes wrong, determine what has changed and how to fix it.

Additionally, building a new image rather than modifying an existing one means the old image is still around, and can quickly be used for a rollback if an error occurs. In contrast, once you copy your new binary over an existing binary, such rollback is nearly impossible.

Immutable container images are at the core of everything that you will build in Kubernetes. It is possible to imperatively change running containers, but this is an antipattern to be used only in extreme cases where there are no other options (e.g., if it is the only way to temporarily repair a mission-critical production system). And even then, the changes must also be recorded through a declarative configuration update at some later time, after the fire is out.

Declarative Configuration

Immutability extends beyond containers running in your cluster to the way you describe your application to Kubernetes. Everything in Kubernetes is a *declarative configuration object* that represents the desired state of the system. It is Kubernetes's job to ensure that the actual state of the world matches this desired state.

Much like mutable versus immutable infrastructure, declarative configuration is an alternative to *imperative* configuration, where the state of the world is defined by the execution of a series of instructions rather than a declaration of the desired state of the world. While imperative commands define actions, declarative configurations define state.

To understand these two approaches, consider the task of producing three replicas of a piece of software. With an imperative approach, the configuration would say: "run A, run B, and run C." The corresponding declarative configuration would be "replicas equals three."

Because it describes the state of the world, declarative configuration does not have to be executed to be understood. Its impact is concretely declared. Since the effects of declarative configuration can be understood before they are executed, declarative configuration is far less error-prone. Further, the traditional tools of software development, such as source control, code review, and unit testing, can be used in declarative configuration in ways that are impossible for imperative instructions.

The combination of declarative state stored in a version control system and Kubernetes's ability to make reality match this declarative state makes rollback of a change trivially easy. It is simply restating the previous declarative state of the system. With imperative systems this is usually impossible, since while the imperative instructions describe how to get you from point A to point B, they rarely include the reverse instructions that can get you back.

Self-Healing Systems

Kubernetes is an online, self-healing system. When it receives a desired state configuration, it does not simply take actions to make the current state match the desired state a single time. It continuously takes actions to ensure that the current state matches the desired state. This means that not only will Kubernetes initialize your system, but it will guard it against any failures or perturbations that might destabilize your system and affect reliability.

A more traditional operator repair involves a manual series of mitigation steps, or human intervention performed in response to some sort of alert. Imperative repair like this is more expensive (since it generally requires an on-call operator to be available to enact the repair). It is also generally slower, since a human must often wake up and log in to respond. Furthermore, it is less reliable since the imperative series of repair operations suffer from all of the problems of imperative management described in the previous section. Self-healing systems like Kubernetes both reduce the burden on operators and improve the overall reliability of the system by performing reliable repairs more quickly.

As a concrete example of this self-healing behavior, if you assert a desired state of three replicas to Kubernetes, it does not just create three replicas—it continuously ensures that there are exactly three replicas. If you manually create a fourth replica Kubernetes will destroy one to bring the number back to three. If you manually destroy a replica, Kubernetes will create one to again return you to the desired state.

Online self-healing systems improve developer velocity because the time and energy you might otherwise have spent on operations and maintenance can instead be spent on developing and testing new features.

Scaling Your Service and Your Teams

As your product grows, its inevitable that you will need to scale both your software and the teams that develop it. Fortunately, Kubernetes can help with both of these goals. Kubernetes achieves scalability by favoring *decoupled* architectures.

Decoupling

In a decoupled architecture each component is separated from other components by defined APIs and service load balancers. APIs and load balancers isolate each piece of the system from the others. APIs provide a buffer between implementer and consumer, and load balancers provide a buffer between running instances of each service.

Decoupling components via load balancers makes it easy to scale the programs that make up your service, because increasing the size (and therefore the capacity) of the program can be done without adjusting or reconfiguring any of the other layers of your service.

Decoupling servers via APIs makes it easier to scale the development teams because each team can focus on a single, smaller *microservice* with a comprehensible surface area. Crisp APIs between microservices limit the amount of cross-team communication overhead required to build and deploy software. This communication overhead is often the major restricting factor when scaling teams.

Easy Scaling for Applications and Clusters

Concretely, when you need to scale your service, the immutable, declarative nature of Kubernetes makes this scaling trivial to implement. Because your containers are immutable, and the number of replicas is simply a number in a declarative config, scaling your service upward is simply a matter of changing a number in a configuration file, asserting this new declarative state to Kubernetes, and letting it take care of the rest. Alternately, you can set up autoscaling and simply let Kubernetes take care of it for you.

Of course, that sort of scaling assumes that there are resources available in your cluster to consume. Sometimes you actually need to scale up the cluster itself. Here again, Kubernetes makes this task easier. Because each machine in a cluster is entirely identical to every other machine, and the applications themselves are decoupled from the details of the machine by containers, adding additional resources to the cluster is simply a matter of imaging a new machine and joining it into the cluster. This can be accomplished via a few simple commands or via a prebaked machine image.

One of the challenges of scaling machine resources is predicting their use. If you are running on physical infrastructure, the time to obtain a new machine is measured in days or weeks. On both physical and cloud infrastructure, predicting future costs is difficult because it is hard to predict the growth and scaling needs of specific applications.

Kubernetes can simplify forecasting future compute costs. To understand why this is true, consider scaling up three teams, A, B, and C. Historically you have seen that each team's growth is highly variable and thus hard to predict. If you are provisioning individual machines for each service, you have no choice but to forecast based on the maximum expected growth for each service, since machines dedicated to one team cannot be used for another team. If instead you use Kubernetes to decouple the teams from the specific machines they are using, you can forecast growth based on the aggregate growth of all three services. Combining three variable growth rates into a single growth rate reduces statistical noise and produces a more reliable forecast of expected growth. Furthermore, decoupling the teams from specific machines means that teams can share fractional parts of each other's machines, reducing even further the overheads associated with forecasting growth of computing resources.

Scaling Development Teams with Microservices

As noted in a variety of research, the ideal team size is the "two-pizza team," or roughly six to eight people, because this group size often results in good knowledge sharing, fast decision making, and a common sense of purpose. Larger teams tend to suffer from hierarchy, poor visibility, and infighting, which hinder agility and success.

However, many projects require significantly more resources to be successful and achieve their goals. Consequently, there is a tension between the ideal team size for agility and the necessary team size for the product's end goals.

The common solution to this tension has been the development of decoupled, service-oriented teams that each build a single microservice. Each small team is responsible for the design and delivery of a service that is consumed by other small teams. The aggregation of all of these services ultimately provides the implementation of the overall product's surface area.

Kubernetes provides numerous abstractions and APIs that make it easier to build these decoupled microservice architectures.

- Pods, or groups of containers, can group together container images developed by different teams into a single deployable unit.
- Kubernetes services provide load balancing, naming, and discovery to isolate one microservice from another.
- Namespaces provide isolation and access control, so that each microservice can control the degree to which other services interact with it.
- Ingress objects provide an easy-to-use frontend that can combine multiple microservices into a single externalized API surface area.

Finally, decoupling the application container image and machine means that different microservices can colocate on the same machine without interfering with each other, reducing the overhead and cost of microservice architectures. The health-checking and rollout features of Kubernetes guarantee a consistent approach to application rollout and reliability that ensures that a proliferation of microservice teams does not also result in a proliferation of different approaches to service production lifecycle and operations.

Separation of Concerns for Consistency and Scaling

In addition to the consistency that Kubernetes brings to operations, the decoupling and separation of concerns produced by the Kubernetes stack lead to significantly greater consistency for the lower levels of your infrastructure. This enables your operations function to scale to managing many machines with a single small, focused team. We have talked at length about the decoupling of application container and machine/operating system (OS), but an important aspect of this decoupling is that the container orchestration API becomes a crisp contract that separates the responsibilities of the application operator from the cluster orchestration operator. We call this the "not my monkey, not my circus" line. The application developer relies on the service-level agreement (SLA) delivered by the container orchestration API, without worrying about the details of how this SLA is achieved. Likewise, the container orchestration API reliability engineer focuses on delivering the orchestration API's SLA without worrying about the applications that are running on top of it.

This decoupling of concerns means that a small team running a Kubernetes cluster can be responsible for supporting hundreds or even thousands of teams running applications within that cluster (Figure 1-1). Likewise, a small team can be responsible for tens (or more) of clusters running around the world. It's important to note that the same decoupling of containers and OS enables the OS reliability engineers to focus on the SLA of the individual machine's OS. This becomes another line of separate responsibility, with the Kubernetes operators relying on the OS SLA, and the OS operators worrying solely about delivering that SLA. Again, this enables you to scale a small team of OS experts to a fleet of thousands of machines.

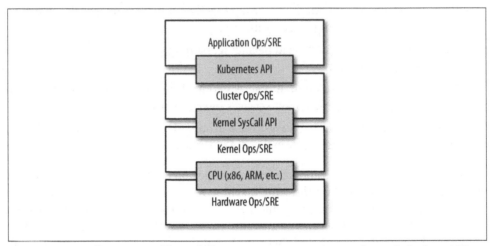

Figure 1-1. An illustration of how different operations teams are decoupled using APIs

Of course, devoting even a small team to managing an OS is beyond the scale of many organizations. In these environments, a managed Kubernetes-as-a-Service (KaaS) provided by a public cloud provider is a great option.

 At the time of writing, you can use managed KaaS on Microsoft Azure, with Azure Container Service, as well as on the Google Cloud Platform via the Google Container Engine (GCE). There is no equivalent service available on Amazon Web Services (AWS), though the kops project provides tools for easy installation and management of Kubernetes on AWS (see "Installing Kubernetes on Amazon Web Services" on page 25).

The decision of whether to use KaaS or manage it yourself is one each user needs to make based on the skills and demands of their situation. Often for small organizations, KaaS provides an easy-to-use solution that enables them to focus their time and energy on building the software to support their work rather than managing a cluster. For a larger organization that can afford a dedicated team for managing its Kubernetes cluster, it may make sense to manage it yourself since it enables greater flexibility in terms of cluster capabilities and operations.

Abstracting Your Infrastructure

The goal of the public cloud is to provide easy-to-use, self-service infrastructure for developers to consume. However, too often cloud APIs are oriented around mirroring the infrastructure that IT expects, not the concepts (e.g., "virtual machines" instead of "applications") that developers want to consume. Additionally, in many cases the cloud comes with particular details in implementation or services that are specific to the cloud provider. Consuming these APIs directly makes it difficult to run your application in multiple environments, or spread between cloud and physical environments.

The move to application-oriented container APIs like Kubernetes has two concrete benefits. First, as we described previously, it separates developers from specific machines. This not only makes the machine-oriented IT role easier, since machines can simply be added in aggregate to scale the cluster, but in the context of the cloud it also enables a high degree of portability since developers are consuming a higher-level API that is implemented in terms of the specific cloud infrastructure APIs.

When your developers build their applications in terms of container images and deploy them in terms of portable Kubernetes APIs, transferring your application between environments, or even running in hybrid environments, is simply a matter of sending the declarative config to a new cluster. Kubernetes has a number of plug-ins that can abstract you from a particular cloud. For example, Kubernetes services know how to create load balancers on all major public clouds as well as several different private and physical infrastructures. Likewise, Kubernetes PersistentVolumes and PersistentVolumeClaims can be used to abstract your applications away from specific storage implementations. Of course, to achieve this portability you need to avoid cloud-managed services (e.g., Amazon's DynamoDB or Google's Cloud Spanner), which means that you will be forced to deploy and manage open source storage solutions like Cassandra, MySQL, or MongoDB.

Putting it all together, building on top of Kubernetes's application-oriented abstractions ensures that the effort that you put into building, deploying, and managing your application is truly portable across a wide variety of environments.

Efficiency

In addition to the developer and IT management benefits that containers and Kubernetes provide, there is also a concrete economic benefit to the abstraction. Because developers no longer think in terms of machines, their applications can be colocated on the same machines without impacting the applications themselves. This means that tasks from multiple users can be packed tightly onto fewer machines.

Efficiency can be measured by the ratio of the useful work performed by a machine or process to the total amount of energy spent doing so. When it comes to deploying and managing applications, many of the available tools and processes (e.g., bash scripts, `apt` updates, or imperative configuration management) are somewhat inefficient. When discussing efficiency it's often helpful to think of both the cost of running a server and the human cost required to manage it.

Running a server incurs a cost based on power usage, cooling requirements, data center space, and raw compute power. Once a server is racked and powered on (or clicked and spun up), the meter literally starts running. Any idle CPU time is money wasted. Thus, it becomes part of the system administrator's responsibilities to keep utilization at acceptable levels, which requires ongoing management. This is where containers and the Kubernetes workflow come in. Kubernetes provides tools that automate the distribution of applications across a cluster of machines, ensuring higher levels of utilization than are possible with traditional tooling.

A further increase in efficiency comes from the fact that a developer's test environment can be quickly and cheaply created as a set of containers running in a personal view of a shared Kubernetes cluster (using a feature called *namespaces*). In the past, turning up a test cluster for a developer might have meant turning up three machines. With Kubernetes it is simple to have all developers share a single test cluster, aggregating their usage onto a much smaller set of machines. Reducing the overall number of machines used in turn drives up the efficiency of each system: since more of the resources (CPU, RAM, etc.) on each individual machine are used, the overall cost of each container becomes much lower.

Reducing the cost of development instances in your stack enables development practices that might previously have been cost-prohibitive. For example, with your application deployed via Kubernetes it becomes conceivable to deploy and test every single commit contributed by every developer throughout your entire stack.

When the cost of each deployment is measured in terms of a small number of containers, rather than multiple complete virtual machines (VMs), the cost you incur for such testing is dramatically lower. Returning to the original value of Kubernetes, this increased testing also increases velocity, since you have both strong signals as to the reliability of your code as well as the granularity of detail required to quickly identify where a problem may have been introduced.

Summary

Kubernetes was built to radically change the way that applications are built and deployed in the cloud. Fundamentally, it was designed to give developers more velocity, efficiency, and agility. We hope the preceding sections have given you an idea of why you should deploy your applications using Kubernetes. Now that you are convinced of that, the following chapters will teach you *how* to deploy your application.

## CHAPTER 2

Creating and Running Containers

Kubernetes is a platform for creating, deploying, and managing distributed applications. These applications come in many different shapes and sizes, but ultimately, they are all comprised of one or more *applications* that run on individual machines. These applications accept input, manipulate data, and then return the results. Before we can even consider building a distributed system, we must first consider how to build the *application container images* that make up the pieces of our distributed system.

Applications are typically comprised of a language runtime, libraries, and your source code. In many cases your application relies on external libraries such as libc and libssl. These external libraries are generally shipped as shared components in the OS that you have installed on a particular machine.

Problems occur when an application developed on a programmer's laptop has a dependency on a shared library that isn't available when the program is rolled out to the production OS. Even when the development and production environments share the exact same version of the OS, problems can occur when developers forget to include dependent asset files inside a package that they deploy to production.

A program can only execute successfully if it can be reliably deployed onto the machine where it should run. Too often the state of the art for deployment involves running imperative scripts, which inevitably have twisty and Byzantine failure cases.

Finally, traditional methods of running multiple applications on a single machine require that all of these programs share the same versions of shared libraries on the system. If the different applications are developed by different teams or organizations, these shared dependencies add needless complexity and coupling between these teams.

In Chapter 1, we argued strongly for the value of immutable images and infrastructure. It turns out that this is exactly the value provided by the container image. As we will see, it easily solves all the problems of dependency management and encapsulation just described.

When working with applications it's often helpful to package them in a way that makes it easy to share them with others. Docker, the default container runtime engine, makes it easy to package an application and push it to a remote registry where it can later be pulled by others.

In this chapter we are going to work with a simple example application that we built for this book to help show this workflow in action. You can find the application on GitHub (*https://github.com/kubernetes-up-and-running/kuard*).

Container images bundle an application and its dependencies, under a root filesystem, into a single artifact. The most popular container image format is the Docker image format, the primary image format supported by Kubernetes. Docker images also include additional metadata used by a container runtime to start a running application instance based on the contents of the container image.

This chapter covers the following topics:

- How to package an application using the Docker image format
- How to start an application using the Docker container runtime

Container Images

For nearly everyone, their first interaction with any container technology is with a container image. A *container image* is a binary package that encapsulates all of the files necessary to run an application inside of an OS container. Depending on how you first experiment with containers, you will either build a container image from your local filesystem or download a preexisting image from a *container registry*. In either case, once the container image is present on your computer, you can run that image to produce a running application inside an OS container.

The Docker Image Format

The most popular and widespread container image format is the Docker image format, which was developed by the Docker open source project for packaging, distributing, and running containers using the `docker` command. Subsequently work has begun by Docker, Inc., and others to standardize the container image format via the Open Container Image (OCI) project. While the OCI set of standards have recently (as of mid-2017) been released as a 1.0 standard, adoption of these standards is still very early. The Docker image format continues to be the de facto standard, and is made up of a series of filesystem layers. Each layer adds, removes, or modifies files from the preceding layer in the filesystem. This is an example of an *overlay* filesystem. There are a variety of different concrete implementations of such filesystems, including `aufs`, `overlay`, and `overlay2`.

Container Layering

Container images are constructed of a series of filesystem layers, where each layer inherits and modifies the layers that came before it. To help explain this in detail, let's build some containers. Note that for correctness the ordering of the layers should be bottom up, but for ease of understanding we take the opposite approach:

```
.
└─ container A: a base operating system only, such as Debian
   └─ container B: build upon #A, by adding Ruby v2.1.10
   └─ container C: build upon #A, by adding Golang v1.6
```

At this point we have three containers: A, B, and C. B and C are *forked* from A and share nothing besides the base container's files. Taking it further, we can build on top of B by adding Rails (version 4.2.6). We may also want to support a legacy application that requires an older version of Rails (e.g., version 3.2.x). We can build a container image to support that application based on B also, planning to someday migrate the app to v4:

```
. (continuing from above)
└─ container B: build upon #A, by adding Ruby v2.1.10
   └─ container D: build upon #B, by adding Rails v4.2.6
   └─ container E: build upon #B, by adding Rails v3.2.x
```

Conceptually, each container image layer builds upon a previous one. Each parent reference is a pointer. While the example here is a simple set of containers, other real-world containers can be part of a larger and extensive directed acyclic graph.

Container images are typically combined with a container configuration file, which provides instructions on how to set up the container environment and execute an application entrypoint. The container configuration often includes information on how to set up networking, namespace isolation, resource constraints (cgroups), and what `syscall` restrictions should be placed on a running container instance. The container root filesystem and configuration file are typically bundled using the Docker image format.

Containers fall into two main categories:

- System containers
- Application containers

System containers seek to mimic virtual machines and often run a full boot process. They often include a set of system services typically found in a VM, such as `ssh`, `cron`, and `syslog`.

Application containers differ from system containers in that they commonly run a single application. While running a single application per container might seem like an unnecessary constraint, it provides the perfect level of granularity for composing scalable applications, and is a design philosophy that is leveraged heavily by pods.

Building Application Images with Docker

In general, container orchestration systems like Kubernetes are focused on building and deploying distributed systems made up of application containers. Consequently, we will focus on application containers for the remainder of this chapter.

Dockerfiles

A Dockerfile can be used to automate the creation of a Docker container image. The following example describes the steps required to build the `kuard` (Kubernetes up and running) image, which is both secure and lightweight in terms of size:

```
FROM alpine
MAINTAINER Kelsey Hightower <kelsey.hightower@kuar.io>
COPY bin/kuard /kuard
ENTRYPOINT ["/kuard"]
```

This text can be stored in a text file, typically named *Dockerfile*, and used to create a Docker image.

Run the following command to create the `kuard` Docker image:

```
$ docker build -t kuard-amd64:1 .
```

We have chosen to build on top of Alpine, an extremely minimal Linux distribution. Consequently, the final image should check in at around 6 MB, which is drastically smaller than many publicly available images that tend to be built on top of more complete OS versions such as Debian.

At this point our `kuard` image lives in the local Docker registry where the image was built and is only accessible to a single machine. The true power of Docker comes from the ability to share images across thousands of machines and the broader Docker community.

Image Security

When it comes to security there are no shortcuts. When building images that will ultimately run in a production Kubernetes cluster, be sure to follow best practices for packaging and distributing applications. For example, don't build containers with passwords baked in—and this includes not just in the final layer, but any layers in the image. One of the counterintuitive problems introduced by container layers is that deleting a file in one layer doesn't delete that file from preceding layers. It still takes up space and it can be accessed by anyone with the right tools—an enterprising attacker can simply create an image that only consists of the layers that contain the password.

Secrets and images should *never* be mixed. If you do so, you will be hacked, and you will bring shame to your entire company or department. We all want to be on TV someday, but there are better ways to go about that.

Optimizing Image Sizes

There are several gotchas that come when people begin to experiment with container images that lead to overly large images. The first thing to remember is that files that are removed by subsequent layers in the system are actually still present in the images; they're just inaccessible. Consider the following situation:

```
.
└─ layer A: contains a large file named 'BigFile'
   └─ layer B: removes 'BigFile'
      └─ layer C: builds on B, by adding a static binary
```

You might think that *BigFile* is no longer present in this image. After all, when you run the image, it is no longer accessible. But in fact it is still present in layer A, which means that whenever you push or pull the image, *BigFile* is still transmitted through the network, even if you can no longer access it.

Another pitfall that people fall into revolves around image caching and building. Remember that each layer is an independent delta from the layer below it. Every time you change a layer, it changes every layer that comes after it. Changing the preceding layers means that they need to be rebuilt, repushed, and repulled to deploy your image to development.

To understand this more fully, consider two images:

```
.
└─ layer A: contains a base OS
   └─ layer B: adds source code server.js
      └─ layer C: installs the 'node' package
```

versus:

```
.
└─ layer A: contains a base OS
   └─ layer B: installs the 'node' package
      └─ layer C: adds source code server.js
```

It seems obvious that both of these images will behave identically, and indeed the first time they are pulled they do. However, consider what happens when *server.js* changes. In one case, it is only the change that needs to be pulled or pushed, but in the other case, both *server.js* and the layer providing the node package need to be pulled and pushed, since the node layer is dependent on the *server.js* layer. In general, you want to order your layers from least likely to change to most likely to change in order to optimize the image size for pushing and pulling.

Storing Images in a Remote Registry

What good is a container image if it's only available on a single machine?

Kubernetes relies on the fact that images described in a pod manifest are available across every machine in the cluster. One option for getting this image to all machines in the cluster would be to export the kuard image and import it on every other machine in the Kubernetes cluster. We can't think of anything more tedious than managing Docker images this way. The process of manually importing and exporting Docker images has human error written all over it. Just say no!

The standard within the Docker community is to store Docker images in a remote registry. There are tons of options when it comes to Docker registries, and what you choose will be largely based on your needs in terms of security requirements and collaboration features.

Generally speaking the first choice you need to make regarding a registry is whether to use a private or a public registry. Public registries allow anyone to download images stored in the registry, while private registries require authentication to download images. In choosing public versus private, it's helpful to consider your use case.

Public registries are great for sharing images with the world, because they allow for easy, unauthenticated use of the container images. You can easily distribute your software as a container image and have confidence that users everywhere will have the exact same experience.

In contrast, a private repository is best for storing your applications that are private to your service and that you don't want the world to use.

Regardless, to push an image, you need to authenticate to the registry. You can generally do this with the docker login command, though there are some differences for certain registries. In the examples here we are pushing to the Google Cloud Platform registry, called the Google Container Registry (GCR). For new users hosting publicly readable images, the Docker Hub (*https://hub.docker.com*) is a great place to start.

Once you are logged in, you can tag the kuard image by prepending the target Docker registry:

```
$ docker tag kuard-amd64:1 gcr.io/kuar-demo/kuard-amd64:1
```

Then you can push the kuard image:

```
$ docker push gcr.io/kuar-demo/kuard-amd64:1
```

Now that the kuard image is available on a remote registry, it's time to deploy it using Docker. Because we pushed it to the public Docker registry, it will be available everywhere without authentication.

The Docker Container Runtime

Kubernetes provides an API for describing an application deployment, but relies on a container runtime to set up an application container using the container-specific APIs native to the target OS. On a Linux system that means configuring cgroups and namespaces.

The default container runtime used by Kubernetes is Docker. Docker provides an API for creating application containers on Linux and Windows systems.

Running Containers with Docker

The Docker CLI tool can be used to deploy containers. To deploy a container from the gcr.io/kuar-demo/kuard-amd64:1 image, run the following command:

```
$ docker run -d --name kuard \
  --publish 8080:8080 \
  gcr.io/kuar-demo/kuard-amd64:1
```

This command starts the kuard database and maps ports 8080 on your local machine to 8080 in the container. This is because each container gets its own IP address, so listening on *localhost* inside the container doesn't cause you to listen on your machine. Without the port forwarding, connections will be inaccessible to your machine.

Exploring the kuard Application

kuard exposes a simple web interface, which can be loaded by pointing your browser at *http://localhost:8080* or via the command line:

```
$ curl http://localhost:8080
```

kuard also exposes a number of interesting functions that we will explore later on in this book.

Limiting Resource Usage

Docker provides the ability to limit the amount of resources used by applications by exposing the underlying cgroup technology provided by the Linux kernel.

Limiting memory resources

One of the key benefits to running applications within a container is the ability to restrict resource utilization. This allows multiple applications to coexist on the same hardware and ensures fair usage.

To limit kuard to 200 MB of memory and 1 GB of swap space, use the `--memory` and `--memory-swap` flags with the `docker run` command.

Stop and remove the current kuard container:

```
$ docker stop kuard
$ docker rm kuard
```

Then start another kuard container using the appropriate flags to limit memory usage:

```
$ docker run -d --name kuard \
  --publish 8080:8080 \
  --memory 200m \
  --memory-swap 1G \
  gcr.io/kuar-demo/kuard-amd64:1
```

Limiting CPU resources

Another critical resource on a machine is the CPU. Restrict CPU utilization using the `--cpu-shares` flag with the `docker run` command:

```
$ docker run -d --name kuard \
  --publish 8080:8080 \
  --memory 200m \
  --memory-swap 1G \
  --cpu-shares 1024 \
  gcr.io/kuar-demo/kuard-amd64:1
```

Cleanup

Once you are done building an image, you can delete it with the `docker rmi` command:

```
docker rmi <tag-name>
```

or

```
docker rmi <image-id>
```

Images can either be deleted via their tag name (e.g., `gcr.io/kuar-demo/kuard-amd64:1`) or via their image ID. As with all ID values in the docker tool, the image ID can be shortened as long as it remains unique. Generally only three or four characters of the ID are necessary.

It's important to note that unless you explicitly delete an image it will live on your system forever, *even* if you build a new image with an identical name. Building this new image simply moves the tag to the new image; it doesn't delete or replace the old image.

Consequently, as you iterate while you are creating a new image, you will often create many, many different images that end up taking up unnecessary space on your computer.

To see the images currently on your machine, you can use the `docker images` command. You can then delete tags you are no longer using.

A slightly more sophisticated approach is to set up a `cron` job to run an image garbage collector. For example, the `docker-gc` tool (*https://github.com/spotify/docker-gc*) is a commonly used image garbage collector that can easily run as a recurring `cron` job, once per day or once per hour, depending on how many images you are creating.

Summary

Application containers provide a clean abstraction for applications, and when packaged in the Docker image format, applications become easy to build, deploy, and distribute. Containers also provide isolation between applications running on the same machine, which helps avoid dependency conflicts. The ability to mount external directories means we can run not only stateless applications in a container, but also applications like `influxdb` that generate lots of data.

## CHAPTER 3

Deploying a Kubernetes Cluster

Now that you have successfully built an application container, you are motivated to learn how to deploy it into a complete reliable, scalable distributed system. Of course, to do that, you need a working Kubernetes cluster. At this point, there are several cloud-based Kubernetes services that make it easy to create a cluster with a few command-line instructions. We highly recommend this approach if you are just getting started with Kubernetes. Even if you are ultimately planning on running Kubernetes on bare metal, it makes sense to quickly get started with Kubernetes, learn about Kubernetes itself, and then learn how to install it on physical machines.

Of course, using a cloud-based solution requires paying for those cloud-based resources as well as having an active network connection to the cloud. For these reasons, local development can be more attractive, and in that case the minikube tool provides an easy-to-use way to get a local Kubernetes cluster up running in a VM on your local laptop or desktop. Though this is attractive, minikube only creates a single-node cluster, which doesn't quite demonstrate all of the aspects of a complete Kubernetes cluster. For that reason, we recommend people start with a cloud-based solution, unless it really doesn't work for their situation. If you truly insist on starting on bare metal, Appendix A at the end of this book gives instructions for building a cluster from a collection of Raspberry Pi single-board computers. These instructions use the kubeadm tool and can be adapted to other machines beyond Raspberry Pis.

Installing Kubernetes on a Public Cloud Provider

This chapter covers installing Kubernetes on the three major cloud providers, Amazon Web Services (AWS), Microsoft Azure, and the Google Cloud Platform.

Google Container Service

The Google Cloud Platform offers a hosted Kubernetes-as-a-Service called Google Container Engine (GKE). To get started with GKE, you need a Google Cloud Platform account with billing enabled and the gcloud tool (*https://cloud.google.com/sdk/downloads*) installed.

Once you have gcloud installed, first set a default zone:

```
$ gcloud config set compute/zone us-west1-a
```

Then you can create a cluster:

```
$ gcloud container clusters create kuar-cluster
```

This will take a few minutes. When the cluster is ready you can get credentials for the cluster using:

```
$ gcloud auth application-default login
```

At this point, you should have a cluster configured and ready to go. Unless you would prefer to install Kubernetes elsewhere, you can skip to "The Kubernetes Client" on page 26.

If you run into trouble, the complete instructions for creating a GKE cluster can be found in the Google Cloud Platform documentation (*http://bit.ly/2ver7Po*).

Installing Kubernetes with Azure Container Service

Microsoft Azure offers a hosted Kubernetes-as-a-Service as part of the Azure Container Service. The easiest way to get started with Azure Container Service is to use the built-in Azure Cloud Shell in the Azure portal. You can activate the shell by clicking the shell icon:

in the upper-right toolbar. The shell has the az tool automatically installed and configured to work with your Azure environment.

Alternatively, you can install the az command-line interface (CLI) on your local machine (*https://github.com/Azure/azure-cli*).

Once you have the shell up and working, you can run:

```
$ az group create --name=kuar --location=westus
```

Once the resource group is created, you can create a cluster using:

```
$ az acs create --orchestrator-type=kubernetes \
  --resource-group=kuar --name=kuar-cluster
```

This will take a few minutes. Once the cluster is created, you can get credentials for the cluster with:

```
$ az acs kubernetes get-credentials --resource-group=kuar --name=kuar-cluster
```

If you don't already have the kubectl tool installed, you can install it using:

```
$ az acs kubernetes install-cli
```

Complete instructions for installing Kubernetes on Azure can be found in the Azure documentation (*http://bit.ly/2veqXYl*).

Installing Kubernetes on Amazon Web Services

AWS does not currently offer hosted Kubernetes service. The landscape for managing Kubernetes on AWS is a fast-evolving area with new and improved tools being introduced often. Here are a couple of options that make it easy to get started:

- The easiest way to launch a small cluster appropriate for exploring Kubernetes with this book is using the Quick Start for Kubernetes by Heptio (*http://amzn.to/2veAy1q*). This is a simple CloudFormation template that can launch a cluster using the AWS Console.

- For a more fully featured management solution, consider using a project called kops. You can find a complete tutorial for installing Kubernetes on AWS using kops on GitHub (*http://bit.ly/2q86l2n*).

Installing Kubernetes Locally Using minikube

If you need a local development experience, or you don't want to pay for cloud resources, you can install a simple single-node cluster using minikube. While mini kube is a good simulation of a Kubernetes cluster, it is really intended for local development, learning, and experimentation. Because it only runs in a VM on a single node, it doesn't provide the reliability of a distributed Kubernetes cluster.

In addition, certain features described in this book require integration with a cloud provider. These features are either not available or work in a limited way with mini kube.

You need to have a hypervisor installed on your machine to use minikube. For Linux and macOS, this is generally virtualbox (*https://virtualbox.org*). On Windows, the Hyper-V hypervisor is the default option. Make sure you install the hypervisor before using minikube.

You can find the minikube tool on GitHub (*https://github.com/kubernetes/minikube*). There are binaries for Linux, macOS, and Windows that you can download. Once you have the minikube tool installed you can create a local cluster using:

```
$ minikube start
```

This will create a local VM, provision Kubernetes, and create a local kubectl configuration that points to that cluster.

When you are done with your cluster, you can stop the VM with:

```
$ minikube stop
```

If you want to remove the cluster, you can run:

```
$ minikube delete
```

Running Kubernetes on Raspberry Pi

If you want to experiment with a realistic Kubernetes cluster but don't want to pay a lot, a very nice Kubernetes cluster can be built on top of Raspberry Pi computers for a relatively small cost. The details of building such a cluster are out of scope for this chapter, but they are given in Appendix A at the end of this book.

The Kubernetes Client

The official Kubernetes client is kubectl: a command-line tool for interacting with the Kubernetes API. kubectl can be used to manage most Kubernetes objects such as pods, ReplicaSets, and services. kubectl can also be used to explore and verify the overall health of the cluster.

We'll use the kubectl tool to explore the cluster you just created.

Checking Cluster Status

The first thing you can do is check the version of the cluster that you are running:

```
$ kubectl version
```

This will display two different versions: the version of the local kubectl tool, as well as the version of the Kubernetes API server.

Don't worry if these versions are different. The Kubernetes tools are backward- and forward-compatible with different versions of the Kubernetes API, so long as you stay within two minor versions of the tools and the cluster and don't try to use newer features on an older cluster. Kubernetes follows the semantic versioning specification, and this minor version is the middle number (e.g., the 5 in 1.5.2).

Now that we've established that you can communicate with your Kubernetes cluster, we'll explore the cluster in more depth.

First, we can get a simple diagnostic for the cluster. This is a good way to verify that your cluster is generally healthy:

```
$ kubectl get componentstatuses
```

The output should look like this:

```
NAME                   STATUS    MESSAGE              ERROR
scheduler              Healthy   ok
controller-manager     Healthy   ok
etcd-0                 Healthy   {"health": "true"}
```

You can see here the components that make up the Kubernetes cluster. The controller-manager is responsible for running various controllers that regulate behavior in the cluster: for example, ensuring that all of the replicas of a service are available and healthy. The scheduler is responsible for placing different pods onto different nodes in the cluster. Finally, the etcd server is the storage for the cluster where all of the API objects are stored.

Listing Kubernetes Worker Nodes

Next, we can list out all of the nodes in our cluster:

```
$ kubectl get nodes
NAME          STATUS         AGE
kubernetes    Ready,master   45d
node-1        Ready          45d
node-2        Ready          45d
node-3        Ready          45d
```

You can see this is a four-node cluster that's been up for 45 days. In Kubernetes nodes are separated into master nodes that contain containers like the API server, scheduler, etc., which manage the cluster, and worker nodes where your containers will run. Kubernetes won't generally schedule work onto master nodes to ensure that user workloads don't harm the overall operation of the cluster.

You can use the kubectl describe command to get more information about a specific node such as node-1:

```
$ kubectl describe nodes node-1
```

First, you see basic information about the node:

```
Name:               node-1
Role:
Labels:             beta.kubernetes.io/arch=arm
                    beta.kubernetes.io/os=linux
                    kubernetes.io/hostname=node-1
```

You can see that this node is running the Linux OS and is running on an ARM processor.

Next, you see information about the operation of node-1 itself:

```
Conditions:
  Type            Status  LastHeartbeatTime    Reason                       Message
  ----            ------  -----------------    ------                       -------
  OutOfDisk       False   Sun, 05 Feb 2017…    KubeletHasSufficientDisk     kubelet…
  MemoryPressure  False   Sun, 05 Feb 2017…    KubeletHasSufficientMemory   kubelet…
  DiskPressure    False   Sun, 05 Feb 2017…    KubeletHasNoDiskPressure     kubelet…
  Ready           True    Sun, 05 Feb 2017…    KubeletReady                 kubelet…
```

These statuses show that the node has sufficient disk and memory space, and it is reporting that it is healthy to the Kubernetes master. Next, there is information about the capacity of the machine:

```
Capacity:
 alpha.kubernetes.io/nvidia-gpu:    0
 cpu:                               4
 memory:                            882636Ki
 pods:                              110
Allocatable:
 alpha.kubernetes.io/nvidia-gpu:    0
 cpu:                               4
 memory:                            882636Ki
 pods:                              110
```

Then, there is information about the software on the node, including the version of Docker running, the versions of Kubernetes and the Linux kernel, and more:

```
System Info:
 Machine ID:                 9989a26f06984d6dbadc01770f018e3b
 System UUID:                9989a26f06984d6dbadc01770f018e3b
 Boot ID:                    98339c67-7924-446c-92aa-c1bfe5d213e6
 Kernel Version:             4.4.39-hypriotos-v7+
 OS Image:                   Raspbian GNU/Linux 8 (jessie)
 Operating System:           linux
 Architecture:               arm
 Container Runtime Version:  docker://1.12.6
 Kubelet Version:            v1.5.2
 Kube-Proxy Version:         v1.5.2
PodCIDR:                     10.244.2.0/24
ExternalID:                  node-1
```

Finally, there is information about the pods that are currently running on this node:

```
Non-terminated Pods:              (3 in total)
  Namespace    Name      CPU Requests CPU Limits Memory Requests Memory Limits
  ---------    ----      ------------ ---------- --------------- -------------
  kube-system  kube-dns… 260m (6%)     0 (0%)     140Mi (16%)     220Mi (25%)
  kube-system  kube-fla… 0 (0%)        0 (0%)     0 (0%)          0 (0%)
  kube-system  kube-pro… 0 (0%)        0 (0%)     0 (0%)          0 (0%)
Allocated resources:
  (Total limits may be over 100 percent, i.e., overcommitted.
  CPU Requests  CPU Limits     Memory Requests Memory Limits
  ------------  ----------     --------------- -------------
  260m (6%)     0 (0%)         140Mi (16%)     220Mi (25%)
No events.
```

From this output you can see the pods on the node (e.g., the kube-dns pod that sup-plies DNS services for the cluster), the CPU and memory that each pod is requesting from the node, as well as the total resources requested. It's worth noting here that Kubernetes tracks both the *request* and upper *limit* for resources for each pod that runs on a machine. The difference between requests and limits is described in detail in Chapter 5, but in a nutshell, resources *requested* by a pod are guaranteed to be present on the node, while a pod's limit is the maximum amount of a given resource that a pod can consume. A pod's limit can be higher than its request, in which case the extra resources are supplied on a best-effort basis. They are not guaranteed to be present on the node.

Cluster Components

One of the interesting aspects of Kubernetes is that many of the components that make up the Kubernetes cluster are actually deployed using Kubernetes itself. We'll take a look at a few of these. These components use a number of the concepts that we'll introduce in later chapters. All of these components run in the kube-system namespace.[1]

Kubernetes Proxy

The Kubernetes proxy is responsible for routing network traffic to load-balanced services in the Kubernetes cluster. To do its job, the proxy must be present on every node in the cluster. Kubernetes has an API object named DaemonSet, which you will learn about later in the book, that is used in many clusters to accomplish this. If your cluster runs the Kubernetes proxy with a DaemonSet, you can see the proxies by run-ning:

---

1 As you'll learn in the next chapter, a namespace in Kubernetes is an entity for organizing Kubernetes resour-ces. You can think of it like a folder in a filesystem.

```
$ kubectl get daemonSets --namespace=kube-system kube-proxy
NAME         DESIRED   CURRENT   READY     NODE-SELECTOR   AGE
kube-proxy   4         4         4         <none>          45d
```

Kubernetes DNS

Kubernetes also runs a DNS server, which provides naming and discovery for the services that are defined in the cluster. This DNS server also runs as a replicated service on the cluster. Depending on the size of your cluster, you may see one or more DNS servers running in your cluster. The DNS service is run as a Kubernetes deployment, which manages these replicas:

```
$ kubectl get deployments --namespace=kube-system kube-dns
NAME       DESIRED   CURRENT   UP-TO-DATE   AVAILABLE   AGE
kube-dns   1         1         1            1           45d
```

There is also a Kubernetes service that performs load-balancing for the DNS server:

```
$ kubectl get services --namespace=kube-system kube-dns
NAME       CLUSTER-IP   EXTERNAL-IP   PORT(S)         AGE
kube-dns   10.96.0.10   <none>        53/UDP,53/TCP   45d
```

This shows that the DNS service for the cluster has the address 10.96.0.10. If you log into a container in the cluster, you'll see that this has been populated into the */etc/resolv.conf* file for the container.

Kubernetes UI

The final Kubernetes component is a GUI. The UI is run as a single replica, but it is still managed by a Kubernetes deployment for reliability and upgrades. You can see this UI server using:

```
$ kubectl get deployments --namespace=kube-system kubernetes-dashboard
NAME                   DESIRED   CURRENT   UP-TO-DATE   AVAILABLE   AGE
kubernetes-dashboard   1         1         1            1           45d
```

The dashboard also has a service that performs load balancing for the dashboard:

```
$ kubectl get services --namespace=kube-system kubernetes-dashboard
NAME                   CLUSTER-IP      EXTERNAL-IP   PORT(S)        AGE
kubernetes-dashboard   10.99.104.174   <nodes>       80:32551/TCP   45d
```

We can use the kubectl proxy to access this UI. Launch the Kubernetes proxy using:

```
$ kubectl proxy
```

This starts up a server running on *localhost:8001*. If you visit *http://localhost:8001/ui* in your web browser, you should see the Kubernetes web UI. You can use this interface to explore your cluster, as well as create new containers. The full details of this interface are outside of the scope of this book, and it is changing rapidly as the dashboard is improved.

Summary

Hopefully at this point you have a Kubernetes cluster (or three) up and running and you've used a few commands to explore the cluster you have created. Next, we'll spend some more time exploring the command-line interface to that Kubernetes cluster and teach you how to master the `kubectl` tool. Throughout the rest of the book, you'll be using `kubectl` and your test cluster to explore the various objects in the Kubernetes API.

## CHAPTER 4

Common kubectl Commands

The `kubectl` command-line utility is a powerful tool, and in the following chapters you will use it to create objects and interact with the Kubernetes API. Before that, however, it makes sense to go over the basic `kubectl` commands that apply to all Kubernetes objects.

Namespaces

Kubernetes uses *namespaces* to organize objects in the cluster. You can think of each namespace as a folder that holds a set of objects. By default, the `kubectl` command-line tool interacts with the `default` namespace. If you want to use a different namespace, you can pass `kubectl` the `--namespace` flag. For example, `kubectl --namespace=mystuff` references objects in the `mystuff` namespace.

Contexts

If you want to change the default namespace more permanently, you can use a *context*. This gets recorded in a `kubectl` configuration file, usually located at `$HOME/.kube/config`. This configuration file also stores how to both find and authenticate to your cluster. For example, you can create a context with a different default namespace for your `kubectl` commands using:

```
$ kubectl config set-context my-context --namespace=mystuff
```

This creates a new context, but it doesn't actually start using it yet. To use this newly created context, you can run:

```
$ kubectl config use-context my-context
```

Contexts can also be used to manage different clusters or different users for authenticating to those clusters using the --users or --clusters flags with the set-context command.

Viewing Kubernetes API Objects

Everything contained in Kubernetes is represented by a RESTful resource. Throughout this book, we refer to these resources as *Kubernetes objects*. Each Kubernetes object exists at a unique HTTP path; for example, *https://your-k8s.com/api/v1/name spaces/default/pods/my-pod* leads to the representation of a pod in the default namespace named my-pod. The kubectl command makes HTTP requests to these URLs to access the Kubernetes objects that reside at these paths.

The most basic command for viewing Kubernetes objects via kubectl is get. If you run *kubectl get <resource-name>* you will get a listing of all resources in the current namespace. If you want to get a specific resource, you can use *kubectl get <resource-name> <object-name>*.

By default, kubectl uses a human-readable printer for viewing the responses from the API server, but this human-readable printer removes many of the details of the objects to fit each object on one terminal line. One way to get slightly more information is to add the -o wide flag, which gives more details, on a longer line. If you want to view the complete object, you can also view the objects as raw JSON or YAML using the -o json or -o yaml flags, respectively.

A common option for manipulating the output of kubectl is to remove the headers, which is often useful when combining kubectl with Unix pipes (e.g., kubectl … | awk …). If you specify the --no-headers flag, kubectl will skip the headers at the top of the human-readable table.

Another common task is extracting specific fields from the object. kubectl uses the JSONPath query language to select fields in the returned object. The complete details of JSONPath are beyond the scope of this chapter, but as an example, this command will extract and print the IP address of the pod:

```
$ kubectl get pods my-pod -o jsonpath --template={.status.podIP}
```

If you are interested in more detailed information about a particular object, use the describe command:

```
$ kubectl describe <resource-name> <obj-name>
```

This will provide a rich multiline human-readable description of the object as well as any other relevant, related objects and events in the Kubernetes cluster.

Creating, Updating, and Destroying Kubernetes Objects

Objects in the Kubernetes API are represented as JSON or YAML files. These files are either returned by the server in response to a query or posted to the server as part of an API request. You can use these YAML or JSON files to create, update, or delete objects on the Kubernetes server.

Let's assume that you have a simple object stored in *obj.yaml*. You can use kubectl to create this object in Kubernetes by running:

```
$ kubectl apply -f obj.yaml
```

Notice that you don't need to specify the resource type of the object; it's obtained from the object file itself.

Similarly, after you make changes to the object, you can use the apply command again to update the object:

```
$ kubectl apply -f obj.yaml
```

> If you feel like making interactive edits, instead of editing a local file, you can instead use the edit command, which will download the latest object state, and then launch an editor that contains the definition:
>
> ```
> $ kubectl edit <resource-name> <obj-name>
> ```
>
> After you save the file, it will be automatically uploaded back to the Kubernetes cluster.

When you want to delete an object, you can simply run:

```
$ kubectl delete -f obj.yaml
```

But it is important to note that kubectl will not prompt you to confirm the delete. Once you issue the command, the object *will* be deleted.

Likewise, you can delete an object using the resource type and name:

```
$ kubectl delete <resource-name> <obj-name>
```

Labeling and Annotating Objects

Labels and annotations are tags for your objects. We'll discuss the differences in Chapter 6, but for now, you can update the labels and annotations on any Kubernetes object using the annotate and label commands. For example, to add the color=red label to a pod named bar, you can run:

```
$ kubectl label pods bar color=red
```

The syntax for annotations is identical.

By default, `label` and `annotate` will not let you overwrite an existing label. To do this, you need to add the `--overwrite` flag.

If you want to remove a label, you can use the `-<label-name>` syntax:

```
$ kubectl label pods bar -color
```

This will remove the `color` label from the pod named `bar`.

Debugging Commands

`kubectl` also makes a number of commands available for debugging your containers. You can use the following to see the logs for a running container:

```
$ kubectl logs <pod-name>
```

If you have multiple containers in your pod you can choose the container to view using the `-c` flag.

By default, `kubectl logs` lists the current logs and exits. If you instead want to continuously stream the logs back to the terminal without exiting, you can add the `-f` (follow) command-line flag.

You can also use the `exec` command to execute a command in a running container:

```
$ kubectl exec -it <pod-name> -- bash
```

This will provide you with an interactive shell inside the running container so that you can perform more debugging.

Finally, you can copy files to and from a container using the `cp` command:

```
$ kubectl cp <pod-name>:/path/to/remote/file /path/to/local/file
```

This will copy a file from a running container to your local machine. You can also specify directories, or reverse the syntax to copy a file from your local machine back out into the container.

Summary

`kubectl` is a powerful tool for managing your applications in your Kubernetes cluster. This chapter has illustrated many of the common uses for the tool, but `kubectl` has a great deal of built-in help available. You can start viewing this help with:

```
kubectl help
```

or:

```
kubectl help command-name
```

## CHAPTER 5

Pods

In earlier chapters we discussed how you might go about containerizing your application, but in real-world deployments of containerized applications you will often want to colocate multiple applications into a single atomic unit, scheduled onto a single machine.

A canonical example of such a deployment is illustrated in Figure 5-1, which consists of a container serving web requests and a container synchronizing the filesystem with a remote Git repository.

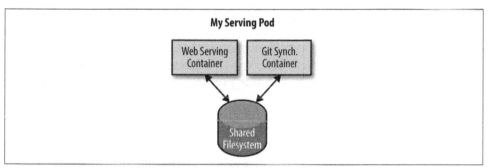

Figure 5-1. An example Pod with two containers and a shared filesystem

At first, it might seem tempting to wrap up both the web server and the Git synchronizer into a single container. After closer inspection, however, the reasons for the separation become clear. First, the two different containers have significantly different requirements in terms of resource usage. Take, for example, memory. Because the web server is serving user requests, we want to ensure that it is always available and responsive. On the other hand, the Git synchronizer isn't really user-facing and has a "best effort" quality of service.

Suppose that our Git synchronizer has a memory leak. We need to ensure that the Git synchronizer cannot use up memory that we want to use for our web server, since this can affect web server performance or even crash the server.

This sort of resource isolation is exactly the sort of thing that containers are designed to accomplish. By separating the two applications into two separate containers we can ensure reliable web server operation.

Of course, the two containers are quite symbiotic; it makes no sense to schedule the web server on one machine and the Git synchronizer on another. Consequently, Kubernetes groups multiple containers into a single, atomic unit called a *Pod*. (The name goes with the whale theme of Docker containers, since a Pod is also a group of whales.)

Pods in Kubernetes

A Pod represents a collection of application containers and volumes running in the same execution environment. Pods, not containers, are the smallest deployable artifact in a Kubernetes cluster. This means all of the containers in a Pod always land on the same machine.

Each container within a Pod runs in its own cgroup, but they share a number of Linux namespaces.

Applications running in the same Pod share the same IP address and port space (network namespace), have the same hostname (UTS namespace), and can communicate using native interprocess communication channels over System V IPC or POSIX message queues (IPC namespace). However, applications in different Pods are isolated from each other; they have different IP addresses, different hostnames, and more. Containers in different Pods running on the same node might as well be on different servers.

Thinking with Pods

One of the most common questions that occurs in the adoption of Kubernetes is "What should I put in a Pod?"

Sometimes people see Pods and think, "Aha! A WordPress container and a MySQL database container should be in the same Pod." However, this kind of Pod is actually an example of an antipattern for Pod construction. There are two reasons for this. First, Wordpress and its database are not truly symbiotic. If the WordPress container and the database container land on different machines, they still can work together quite effectively, since they communicate over a network connection. Secondly, you don't necessarily want to scale WordPress and the database as a unit. WordPress itself is mostly stateless, and thus you may want to scale your WordPress frontends in response to frontend load by creating more WordPress Pods. Scaling a MySQL database is much trickier, and you would be much more likely to increase the resources dedicated to a single MySQL Pod. If you group the WordPress and MySQL containers together in a single Pod, you are forced to use the same scaling strategy for both containers, which doesn't fit well.

In general, the right question to ask yourself when designing Pods is, "Will these containers work correctly if they land on different machines?" If the answer is "no," a Pod is the correct grouping for the containers. If the answer is "yes," multiple Pods is probably the correct solution. In the example at the beginning of this chapter, the two containers interact via a local filesystem. It would be impossible for them to operate correctly if the containers were scheduled on different machines.

In the remaining sections of this chapter, we will describe how to create, introspect, manage, and delete Pods in Kubernetes.

The Pod Manifest

Pods are described in a Pod manifest. The Pod manifest is just a text-file representation of the Kubernetes API object. Kubernetes strongly believes in *declarative configuration*. Declarative configuration means that you write down the desired state of the world in a configuration and then submit that configuration to a service that takes actions to ensure the desired state becomes the actual state.

Declarative configuration is different from *imperative configuration*, where you simply take a series of actions (e.g., apt-get install foo) to modify the world. Years of production experience have taught us that maintaining a written record of the system's desired state leads to a more manageable, reliable system. Declarative configuration enables numerous advantages, including code review for configurations as well as documenting the current state of the world for distributed teams. Additionally, it is the basis for all of the self-healing behaviors in Kubernetes that keep applications running without user action.

The Kubernetes API server accepts and processes Pod manifests before storing them in persistent storage (etcd). The scheduler also uses the Kubernetes API to find Pods that haven't been scheduled to a node. The scheduler then places the Pods onto nodes depending on the resources and other constraints expressed in the Pod manifests. Multiple Pods can be placed on the same machine as long as there are sufficient resources. However, scheduling multiple replicas of the same application onto the same machine is worse for reliability, since the machine is a single failure domain. Consequently, the Kubernetes scheduler tries to ensure that Pods from the same application are distributed onto different machines for reliability in the presence of such failures. Once scheduled to a node, Pods don't move and must be explicitly destroyed and rescheduled.

Multiple instances of a Pod can be deployed by repeating the workflow described here. However, ReplicaSets (Chapter 8) are better suited for running multiple instances of a Pod. (It turns out they're also better at running a single Pod, but we'll get into that later.)

Creating a Pod

The simplest way to create a Pod is via the imperative `kubectl run` command. For example, to run our same kuard server, use:

```
$ kubectl run kuard --image=gcr.io/kuar-demo/kuard-amd64:1
```

You can see the status of this Pod by running:

```
$ kubectl get pods
```

You may initially see the container as `Pending`, but eventually you will see it transition to `Running`, which means that the Pod and its containers have been successfully created.

Don't worry too much about the random strings attached to the end of the Pod name. This manner of creating a Pod actually creates it via `Deployment` and `ReplicaSet` objects, which we will cover in later chapters.

For now, you can delete this Pod by running:

```
$ kubectl delete deployments/kuard
```

We will now move on to writing a complete Pod manifest by hand.

Creating a Pod Manifest

Pod manifests can be written using YAML or JSON, but YAML is generally preferred because it is slightly more human-editable and has the ability to add comments. Pod manifests (and other Kubernetes API objects) should really be treated in the same way as source code, and things like comments help explain the Pod to new team members who are looking at them for the first time.

Pod manifests include a couple of key fields and attributes: mainly a `metadata` section for describing the Pod and its labels, a `spec` section for describing volumes, and a list of containers that will run in the Pod.

In Chapter 2 we deployed kuard using the following Docker command:

```
$ docker run -d --name kuard \
  --publish 8080:8080 \
  gcr.io/kuar-demo/kuard-amd64:1
```

A similar result can be achieved by instead writing Example 5-1 to a file named *kuard-pod.yaml* and then using `kubectl` commands to load that manifest to Kubernetes.

Example 5-1. kuard-pod.yaml

```
apiVersion: v1
kind: Pod
metadata:
  name: kuard
spec:
  containers:
    - image: gcr.io/kuar-demo/kuard-amd64:1
      name: kuard
      ports:
        - containerPort: 8080
          name: http
          protocol: TCP
```

Running Pods

In the previous section we created a Pod manifest that can be used to start a Pod running kuard. Use the `kubectl apply` command to launch a single instance of kuard:

```
$ kubectl apply -f kuard-pod.yaml
```

The Pod manifest will be submitted to the Kubernetes API server. The Kubernetes system will then schedule that Pod to run on a healthy node in the cluster, where it will be monitored by the `kubelet` daemon process. Don't worry if you don't understand all the moving parts of Kubernetes right now; we'll get into more details throughout the book.

Listing Pods

Now that we have a Pod running, let's go find out some more about it. Using the kubectl command-line tool, we can list all Pods running in the cluster. For now, this should only be the single Pod that we created in the previous step:

```
$ kubectl get pods
NAME       READY     STATUS    RESTARTS   AGE
kuard      1/1       Running   0          44s
```

You can see the name of the Pod (kuard) that we gave it in the previous YAML file. In addition to the number of ready containers (1/1), the output also shows the status, the number of times the Pod was restarted, as well as the age of the Pod.

If you ran this command immediately after the Pod was created, you might see:

```
NAME      READY    STATUS     RESTARTS   AGE
kuard     0/1      Pending    0          1s
```

The `Pending` state indicates that the Pod has been submitted but hasn't been scheduled yet.

If a more significant error occurs (e.g., an attempt to create a Pod with a container
image that doesn't exist), it will also be listed in the status field.

 By default, the `kubectl` command-line tool tries to be concise in
the information it reports, but you can get more information via
command-line flags. Adding `-o wide` to any `kubectl` command
will print out slightly more information (while still trying to keep
the information to a single line). Adding `-o json` or `-o yaml` will
print out the complete objects in JSON or YAML, respectively.

Pod Details

Sometimes, the single-line view is insufficient because it is too terse. Additionally,
Kubernetes maintains numerous events about Pods that are present in the event
stream, not attached to the Pod object.

To find out more information about a Pod (or any Kubernetes object) you can use the
`kubectl describe` command. For example, to describe the Pod we previously created, you can run:

```
$ kubectl describe pods kuard
```

This outputs a bunch of information about the Pod in different sections. At the top is
basic information about the Pod:

```
Name:          kuard
Namespace:     default
Node:          node1/10.0.15.185
Start Time:    Sun, 02 Jul 2017 15:00:38 -0700
Labels:        <none>
Annotations:   <none>
Status:        Running
IP:            192.168.199.238
Controllers:   <none>
```

Then there is information about the containers running in the Pod:

```
Containers:
  kuard:
    Container ID:  docker://055095…
    Image:         gcr.io/kuar-demo/kuard-amd64:1
    Image ID:      docker-pullable://gcr.io/kuar-demo/kuard-amd64@sha256:a580…
    Port:          8080/TCP
    State:         Running
      Started:     Sun, 02 Jul 2017 15:00:41 -0700
```

```
    Ready:         True
    Restart Count: 0
    Environment:   <none>
    Mounts:
      /var/run/secrets/kubernetes.io/serviceaccount from default-token-cg5f5 (ro)
```

Finally, there are events related to the Pod, such as when it was scheduled, when its image was pulled, and if/when it had to be restarted because of failing health checks:

```
Events:
  Seen  From               SubObjectPath         Type     Reason     Message
  ----  ----               -------------         -------- ------     -------
  50s   default-scheduler                        Normal   Scheduled  Success…
  49s   kubelet, node1     spec.containers{kuard} Normal   Pulling    pulling
  47s   kubelet, node1     spec.containers{kuard} Normal   Pulled     Success…
  47s   kubelet, node1     spec.containers{kuard} Normal   Created    Created…
  47s   kubelet, node1     spec.containers{kuard} Normal   Started    Started…
```

Deleting a Pod

When it is time to delete a Pod, you can delete it either by name:

```
$ kubectl delete pods/kuard
```

or using the same file that you used to create it:

```
$ kubectl delete -f kuard-pod.yaml
```

When a Pod is deleted, it is *not* immediately killed. Instead, if you run kubectl get pods you will see that the Pod is in the Terminating state. All Pods have a termination *grace period*. By default, this is 30 seconds. When a Pod is transitioned to Terminating it no longer receives new requests. In a serving scenario, the grace period is important for reliability because it allows the Pod to finish any active requests that it may be in the middle of processing before it is terminated.

It's important to note that when you delete a Pod, any data stored in the containers associated with that Pod will be deleted as well. If you want to persist data across multiple instances of a Pod, you need to use PersistentVolumes, described at the end of this chapter.

Accessing Your Pod

Now that your Pod is running, you're going to want to access it for a variety of reasons. You may want to load the web service that is running in the Pod. You may want to view its logs to debug a problem that you are seeing, or even execute other commands in the context of the Pod to help debug. The following sections detail various ways that you can interact with the code and data running inside your Pod.

Using Port Forwarding

Later in the book, we'll show how to expose a service to the world or other containers using load balancers, but oftentimes you simply want to access a specific Pod, even if it's not serving traffic on the internet.

To achieve this, you can use the port-forwarding support built into the Kubernetes API and command-line tools.

When you run:

```
$ kubectl port-forward kuard 8080:8080
```

a secure tunnel is created from your local machine, through the Kubernetes master, to the instance of the Pod running on one of the worker nodes.

As long as the port-forward command is still running, you can access the Pod (in this case the kuard web interface) on *http://localhost:8080*.

Getting More Info with Logs

When your application needs debugging, it's helpful to be able to dig deeper than describe to understand what the application is doing. Kubernetes provides two commands for debugging running containers. The kubectl logs command downloads the current logs from the running instance:

```
$ kubectl logs kuard
```

Adding the -f flag will cause you to continuously stream logs.

The kubectl logs command always tries to get logs from the currently running container. Adding the --previous flag will get logs from a previous instance of the container. This is useful, for example, if your containers are continuously restarting due to a problem at container startup.

 While using kubectl logs is useful for one-off debugging of containers in production environments, it's generally useful to use a log aggregation service. There are several open source log aggregation tools, like fluentd and elasticsearch, as well as numerous cloud logging providers. Log aggregation services provide greater capacity for storing a longer duration of logs, as well as rich log searching and filtering capabilities. Finally, they often provide the ability to aggregate logs from multiple Pods into a single view.

Running Commands in Your Container with exec

Sometimes logs are insufficient, and to truly determine what's going on you need to execute commands in the context of the container itself. To do this you can use:

```
$ kubectl exec kuard date
```

You can also get an interactive session by adding the -it flags:

```
$ kubectl exec -it kuard ash
```

Copying Files to and from Containers

At times you may need to copy files from a remote container to a local machine for more in-depth exploration. For example, you can use a tool like Wireshark to visualize tcpdump packet captures. Suppose you had a file called */captures/capture3.txt* inside a container in your Pod. You could securely copy that file to your local machine by running:

```
$ kubectl cp <pod-name>:/captures/capture3.txt ./capture3.txt
```

Other times you may need to copy files from your local machine into a container. Let's say you want to copy *$HOME/config.txt* to a remote container. In this case, you can run:

```
$ kubectl cp $HOME/config.txt <pod-name>:/config.txt
```

Generally speaking, copying files into a container is an antipattern. You really should treat the contents of a container as immutable. But occasionally it's the most immediate way to stop the bleeding and restore your service to health, since it is quicker than building, pushing, and rolling out a new image. Once the bleeding is stopped, however, it is critically important that you immediately go and do the image build and rollout, or you are guaranteed to forget the local change that you made to your container and overwrite it in the subsequent regularly scheduled rollout.

Health Checks

When you run your application as a container in Kubernetes, it is automatically kept alive for you using a *process health check*. This health check simply ensures that the main process of your application is always running. If it isn't, Kubernetes restarts it.

However, in most cases, a simple process check is insufficient. For example, if your process has deadlocked and is unable to serve requests, a process health check will still believe that your application is healthy since its process is still running.

To address this, Kubernetes introduced health checks for application *liveness*. Liveness health checks run application-specific logic (e.g., loading a web page) to verify that the application is not just still running, but is functioning properly. Since these liveness health checks are application-specific, you have to define them in your Pod manifest.

Liveness Probe

Once the kuard process is up and running, we need a way to confirm that it is actually healthy and shouldn't be restarted. Liveness probes are defined per container, which means each container inside a Pod is health-checked separately. In Example 5-2, we add a liveness probe to our kuard container, which runs an HTTP request against the /healthy path on our container.

Example 5-2. kuard-pod-health.yaml

```
apiVersion: v1
kind: Pod
metadata:
  name: kuard
spec:
  containers:
    - image: gcr.io/kuar-demo/kuard-amd64:1
      name: kuard
      livenessProbe:
        httpGet:
          path: /healthy
          port: 8080
        initialDelaySeconds: 5
        timeoutSeconds: 1
        periodSeconds: 10
        failureThreshold: 3
      ports:
        - containerPort: 8080
          name: http
          protocol: TCP
```

The preceding Pod manifest uses an httpGet probe to perform an HTTP GET request against the /healthy endpoint on port 8080 of the kuard container. The probe sets an initialDelaySeconds of 5, and thus will not be called until five seconds after all the containers in the Pod are created. The probe must respond within the one-second timeout, and the HTTP status code must be equal to or greater than 200 and less than 400 to be considered successful. Kubernetes will call the probe every 10 seconds. If more than three probes fail, the container will fail and restart.

You can see this in action by looking at the kuard status page. Create a Pod using this manifest and then port-forward to that Pod:

```
$ kubectl apply -f kuard-pod-health.yaml
$ kubectl port-forward kuard 8080:8080
```

Point your browser to *http://localhost:8080*. Click the "Liveness Probe" tab. You should see a table that lists all of the probes that this instance of kuard has received. If you click the "fail" link on that page, kuard will start to fail health checks. Wait long

---

enough and Kubernetes will restart the container. At that point the display will reset and start over again. Details of the restart can be found with kubectl describe kuard. The "Events" section will have text similar to the following:

```
Killing container with id docker://2ac946...:pod "kuard_default(9ee84...)"
container "kuard" is unhealthy, it will be killed and re-created.
```

Readiness Probe

Of course, liveness isn't the only kind of health check we want to perform. Kubernetes makes a distinction between *liveness* and *readiness*. Liveness determines if an application is running properly. Containers that fail liveness checks are restarted. Readiness describes when a container is ready to serve user requests. Containers that fail readiness checks are removed from service load balancers. Readiness probes are configured similarly to liveness probes. We explore Kubernetes services in detail in Chapter 7.

Combining the readiness and liveness probes helps ensure only healthy containers are running within the cluster.

Types of Health Checks

In addition to HTTP checks, Kubernetes also supports tcpSocket health checks that open a TCP socket; if the connection is successful, the probe succeeds. This style of probe is useful for non-HTTP applications; for example, databases or other non–HTTP-based APIs.

Finally, Kubernetes allows exec probes. These execute a script or program in the context of the container. Following typical convention, if this script returns a zero exit code, the probe succeeds; otherwise, it fails. exec scripts are often useful for custom application validation logic that doesn't fit neatly into an HTTP call.

Resource Management

Most people move into containers and orchestrators like Kubernetes because of the radical improvements in image packaging and reliable deployment they provide. In addition to application-oriented primitives that simplify distributed system development, equally important is the ability to increase the overall utilization of the compute nodes that make up the cluster. The basic cost of operating a machine, either virtual or physical, is basically constant regardless of whether it is idle or fully loaded. Consequently, ensuring that these machines are maximally active increases the efficiency of every dollar spent on infrastructure.

Generally speaking, we measure this efficiency with the *utilization* metric. Utilization is defined as the amount of a resource actively being used divided by the amount of a resource that has been purchased. For example, if you purchase a one-core machine, and your application uses one-tenth of a core, then your utilization is 10%.

With scheduling systems like Kubernetes managing resource packing, you can drive your utilization to greater than 50%.

To achieve this, you have to tell Kubernetes about the resources your application requires, so that Kubernetes can find the optimal packing of containers onto purchased machines.

Kubernetes allows users to specify two different resource metrics. Resource *requests* specify the minimum amount of a resource required to run the application. Resource *limits* specify the maximum amount of a resource that an application can consume. Both of these resource definitions are described in greater detail in the following sections.

Resource Requests: Minimum Required Resources

With Kubernetes, a Pod requests the resources required to run its containers. Kubernetes guarantees that these resources are available to the Pod. The most commonly requested resources are CPU and memory, but Kubernetes has support for other resource types as well, such as GPUs and more.

For example, to request that the kuard container lands on a machine with half a CPU free and gets 128 MB of memory allocated to it, we define the Pod as shown in Example 5-3.

Example 5-3. kuard-pod-resreq.yaml

```
apiVersion: v1
kind: Pod
metadata:
  name: kuard
spec:
  containers:
    - image: gcr.io/kuar-demo/kuard-amd64:1
      name: kuard
      resources:
        requests:
          cpu: "500m"
          memory: "128Mi"
      ports:
        - containerPort: 8080
          name: http
          protocol: TCP
```

Resources are requested per container, not per Pod. The total resources requested by the Pod is the sum of all resources requested by all containers in the Pod. The reason for this is that in many cases the different containers have very different CPU requirements. For example, in the web server and data synchronizer Pod, the web server is user-facing and likely needs a great deal of CPU, while the data synchronizer can make do with very little.

Request limit details

Requests are used when scheduling Pods to nodes. The Kubernetes scheduler will ensure that the sum of all requests of all Pods on a node does not exceed the capacity of the node. Therefore, a Pod is guaranteed to have at least the requested resources when running on the node. Importantly, "request" specifies a minimum. It does not specify a maximum cap on the resources a Pod may use. To explore what this means, let's look at an example.

Imagine that we have container whose code attempts to use all available CPU cores. Suppose that we create a Pod with this container that requests 0.5 CPU. Kubernetes schedules this Pod onto a machine with a total of 2 CPU cores.

As long as it is the only Pod on the machine, it will consume all 2.0 of the available cores, despite only requesting 0.5 CPU.

If a second Pod with the same container and the same request of 0.5 CPU lands on the machine, then each Pod will receive 1.0 cores.

If a third identical Pod is scheduled, each Pod will receive 0.66 cores. Finally, if a fourth identical Pod is scheduled, each Pod will receive the 0.5 core it requested, and the node will be at capacity.

CPU requests are implemented using the `cpu-shares` functionality in the Linux kernel.

Memory requests are handled similarly to CPU, but there is an important difference. If a container is over its memory request, the OS can't just remove memory from the process, because it's been allocated. Consequently, when the system runs out of memory, the `kubelet` terminates containers whose memory usage is greater than their requested memory. These containers are automatically restarted, but with less available memory on the machine for the container to consume.

Since resource requests guarantee resource availability to a Pod, they are critical to ensuring that containers have sufficient resources in high-load situations.

Capping Resource Usage with Limits

In addition to setting the resources required by a Pod, which establishes the minimum resources available to the Pod, you can also set a maximum on a Pod's resource usage via resource *limits*.

In our previous example we created a kuard Pod that requested a minimum of 0.5 of a core and 128 MB of memory. In the Pod manifest in Example 5-4, we extend this configuration to add a limit of 1.0 CPU and 256 MB of memory.

Example 5-4. kuard-pod-reslim.yaml

```
apiVersion: v1
kind: Pod
metadata:
  name: kuard
spec:
  containers:
    - image: gcr.io/kuar-demo/kuard-amd64:1
      name: kuard
      resources:
        requests:
          cpu: "500m"
          memory: "128Mi"
        limits:
          cpu: "1000m"
          memory: "256Mi"
      ports:
        - containerPort: 8080
          name: http
          protocol: TCP
```

When you establish limits on a container, the kernel is configured to ensure that consumption cannot exceed these limits. A container with a CPU limit of 0.5 cores will only ever get 0.5 cores, even if the CPU is otherwise idle. A container with a memory limit of 256 MB will not be allowed additional memory (e.g., malloc will fail) if its memory usage exceeds 256 MB.

Persisting Data with Volumes

When a Pod is deleted or a container restarts, any and all data in the container's filesystem is also deleted. This is often a good thing, since you don't want to leave around cruft that happened to be written by your stateless web application. In other cases, having access to persistent disk is an important part of a healthy application. Kubernetes models such persistent storage.

Using Volumes with Pods

To add a volume to a Pod manifest, there are two new stanzas to add to our configuration. The first is a new `spec.volumes` section. This array defines all of the volumes that may be accessed by containers in the Pod manifest. It's important to note that not all containers are required to mount all volumes defined in the Pod. The second addition is the `volumeMounts` array in the container definition. This array defines the volumes that are mounted into a particular container, and the path where each volume should be mounted. Note that two different containers in a Pod can mount the same volume at different mount paths.

The manifest in Example 5-5 defines a single new volume named `kuard-data`, which the `kuard` container mounts to the `/data` path.

Example 5-5. kuard-pod-vol.yaml

```
apiVersion: v1
kind: Pod
metadata:
  name: kuard
spec:
  volumes:
    - name: "kuard-data"
      hostPath:
        path: "/var/lib/kuard"
  containers:
    - image: gcr.io/kuar-demo/kuard-amd64:1
      name: kuard
      volumeMounts:
        - mountPath: "/data"
          name: "kuard-data"
      ports:
        - containerPort: 8080
          name: http
          protocol: TCP
```

Different Ways of Using Volumes with Pods

There are a variety of ways you can use data in your application. The following are a few, and the recommended patterns for Kubernetes.

Communication/synchronization

In the first example of a Pod, we saw how two containers used a shared volume to serve a site while keeping it synchronized to a remote Git location. To achieve this, the Pod uses an `emptyDir` volume. Such a volume is scoped to the Pod's lifespan, but it can be shared between two containers, forming the basis for communication between our Git sync and web serving containers.

Cache

An application may use a volume that is valuable for performance, but not required for correct operation of the application. For example, perhaps the application keeps prerendered thumbnails of larger images. Of course, they can be reconstructed from the original images, but that makes serving the thumbnails more expensive. You want such a cache to survive a container restart due to a health check failure, and thus emptyDir works well for the cache use case as well.

Persistent data

Sometimes you will use a volume for truly persistent data—data that is independent of the lifespan of a particular Pod, and should move between nodes in the cluster if a node fails or a Pod moves to a different machine for some reason. To achieve this, Kubernetes supports a wide variety of remote network storage volumes, including widely supported protocols like NFS or iSCSI as well as cloud provider network storage like Amazon's Elastic Block Store, Azure's Files and Disk Storage, as well as Google's Persistent Disk.

Mounting the host filesystem

Other applications don't actually need a persistent volume, but they do need some access to the underlying host filesystem. For example, they may need access to the */dev* filesystem in order to perform raw block-level access to a device on the system. For these cases, Kubernetes supports the hostDir volume, which can mount arbitrary locations on the worker node into the container.

The previous example uses the hostDir volume type. The volume created is */var/lib/kuard* on the host.

Persisting Data Using Remote Disks

Oftentimes, you want the data a Pod is using to stay with the Pod, even if it is restarted on a different host machine.

To achieve this, you can mount a remote network storage volume into your Pod. When using network-based storage, Kubernetes automatically mounts and unmounts the appropriate storage whenever a Pod using that volume is scheduled onto a particular machine.

There are numerous methods for mounting volumes over the network. Kubernetes includes support for standard protocols such as NFS and iSCSI as well as cloud provider–based storage APIs for the major cloud providers (both public and private). In many cases, the cloud providers will also create the disk for you if it doesn't already exist.

Here is an example of using an NFS server:

```
...
# Rest of pod definition above here
volumes:
  - name: "kuard-data"
    nfs:
      server: my.nfs.server.local
      path: "/exports"
```

Putting It All Together

Many applications are stateful, and as such we must preserve any data and ensure access to the underlying storage volume regardless of what machine the application runs on. As we saw earlier, this can be achieved using a persistent volume backed by network-attached storage. We also want to ensure a healthy instance of the application is running at all times, which means we want to make sure the container running kuard is ready before we expose it to clients.

Through a combination of persistent volumes, readiness and liveness probes, and resource restrictions Kubernetes provides everything needed to run stateful applications reliably. Example 5-6 pulls this all together into one manifest.

Example 5-6. kuard-pod-full.yaml

```
apiVersion: v1
kind: Pod
metadata:
  name: kuard
spec:
  volumes:
    - name: "kuard-data"
      nfs:
        server: my.nfs.server.local
        path: "/exports"
  containers:
    - image: gcr.io/kuar-demo/kuard-amd64:1
      name: kuard
      ports:
        - containerPort: 8080
          name: http
          protocol: TCP
      resources:
        requests:
          cpu: "500m"
          memory: "128Mi"
        limits:
          cpu: "1000m"
          memory: "256Mi"
      volumeMounts:
        - mountPath: "/data"
```

```
        name: "kuard-data"
    livenessProbe:
      httpGet:
        path: /healthy
        port: 8080
      initialDelaySeconds: 5
      timeoutSeconds: 1
      periodSeconds: 10
      failureThreshold: 3
    readinessProbe:
      httpGet:
        path: /ready
        port: 8080
      initialDelaySeconds: 30
      timeoutSeconds: 1
      periodSeconds: 10
      failureThreshold: 3
```

Persistent volumes are a deep topic that has many different details: in particular, the manner in which persistent volumes, persistent volume claims, and dynamic volume provisioning work together. There is a more in-depth examination of the subject in Chapter 13.

Summary

Pods represent the atomic unit of work in a Kubernetes cluster. Pods are comprised of one or more containers working together symbiotically. To create a Pod, you write a Pod manifest and submit it to the Kubernetes API server by using the command-line tool or (less frequently) by making HTTP and JSON calls to the server directly.

Once you've submitted the manifest to the API server, the Kubernetes scheduler finds a machine where the Pod can fit and schedules the Pod to that machine. Once scheduled, the kubelet daemon on that machine is responsible for creating the containers that correspond to the Pod, as well as performing any health checks defined in the Pod manifested.

Once a Pod is scheduled to a node, no rescheduling occurs if that node fails. Additionally, to create multiple replicas of the same Pod you have to create and name them manually. In a later chapter we introduce the ReplicaSet object and show how you can automate the creation of multiple identical Pods and ensure that they are recreated in the event of a node machine failure.

## CHAPTER 6

Labels and Annotations

Kubernetes was made to grow with you as your application scales both in size and complexity. With this in mind, labels and annotations were added as foundational concepts. Labels and annotations let you work in sets of things that map to how *you* think about your application. You can organize, mark, and cross-index all of your resources to represent the groups that make the most sense for your application.

Labels are key/value pairs that can be attached to Kubernetes objects such as Pods and ReplicaSets. They can be arbitrary, and are useful for attaching identifying information to Kubernetes objects. Labels provide the foundation for grouping objects.

Annotations, on the other hand, provide a storage mechanism that resembles labels: annotations are key/value pairs designed to hold nonidentifying information that can be leveraged by tools and libraries.

Labels

Labels provide identifying metadata for objects. These are fundamental qualities of the object that will be used for grouping, viewing, and operating.

The motivations for labels grew out of Google's experience in running large and complex applications. There were a couple of lessons that emerged from this experience. See the great *Site Reliability Engineering* by Betsy Beyer et al. (O'Reilly) for some deeper background on how Google approaches production systems.

The first lesson is that production abhors a singleton. When deploying software, users will often start with a single instance. However, as the application matures, these singletons often multiply and become sets of objects. With this in mind, Kubernetes uses labels to deal with *sets* of objects instead of single instances.

The second lesson is that any hierarchy imposed by the system will fall short for many users. In addition, user grouping and hierarchy are subject to change over time. For instance, a user may start out with the idea that all apps are made up of many services. However, over time, a service may be shared across multiple apps. Kubernetes labels are flexible enough to adapt to these situations and more.

Labels have simple syntax. They are key/value pairs where both the key and value are represented by strings. Label keys can be broken down into two parts: an optional prefix and a name, separated by a slash. The prefix, if specified, must be a DNS subdomain with a 253-character limit. The key name is required and must be shorter than 63 characters. Names must also start and end with an alphanumeric character and permit the use of dashes (-), underscores (_), and dots (.) between characters.

Label values are strings with a maximum length of 63 characters. The contents of the label values follow the same rules as for label keys.

Table 6-1 shows valid label keys and values.

Table 6-1. Label examples

Key	Value
acme.com/app-version	1.0.0
appVersion	1.0.0
app.version	1.0.0
kubernetes.io/cluster-service	true

Applying Labels

Here we create a few deployments (a way to create an array of Pods) with some interesting labels. We'll take two apps (called `alpaca` and `bandicoot`) and have two environments for each. We will also have two different versions.

1. First, create the `alpaca-prod` deployment and set the ver, app, and env labels:

```
$ kubectl run alpaca-prod \
  --image=gcr.io/kuar-demo/kuard-amd64:1 \
  --replicas=2 \
  --labels="ver=1,app=alpaca,env=prod"
```

2. Next, create the `alpaca-test` deployment and set the ver, app, and env labels with the appropriate values:

```
$ kubectl run alpaca-test \
  --image=gcr.io/kuar-demo/kuard-amd64:2 \
  --replicas=1 \
  --labels="ver=2,app=alpaca,env=test"
```

3. Finally, create two deployments for bandicoot. Here we name the environments prod and staging:

```
$ kubectl run bandicoot-prod \
  --image=gcr.io/kuar-demo/kuard-amd64:2 \
  --replicas=2 \
  --labels="ver=2,app=bandicoot,env=prod"
$ kubectl run bandicoot-staging \
  --image=gcr.io/kuar-demo/kuard-amd64:2 \
  --replicas=1 \
  --labels="ver=2,app=bandicoot,env=staging"
```

At this point you should have four deployments—alpaca-prod, alpaca-staging, bandicoot-prod, and bandicoot-staging:

```
$ kubectl get deployments --show-labels

NAME                ... LABELS
alpaca-prod         ... app=alpaca,env=prod,ver=1
alpaca-test         ... app=alpaca,env=test,ver=2
bandicoot-prod      ... app=bandicoot,env=prod,ver=2
bandicoot-staging   ... app=bandicoot,env=staging,ver=2
```

We can visualize this as a Venn diagram based on the labels (Figure 6-1).

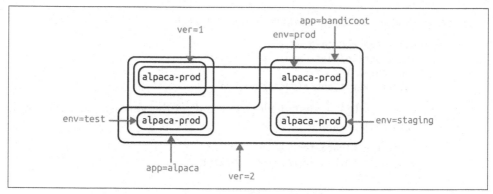

Figure 6-1. Visualization of labels applied to our deployments

Modifying Labels

Labels can also be applied (or updated) on objects after they are created.

```
$ kubectl label deployments alpaca-test "canary=true"
```

There is a caveat to be aware of here. In this example, the kubectl label command will only change the label on the deployment itself; it won't affect the objects (ReplicaSets and Pods) the deployment creates. To change those, you'll need to change the template embedded in the deployment (see Chapter 12).

You can also use the -L option to kubectl get to show a label value as a column:

```
$ kubectl get deployments -L canary
```

```
NAME                DESIRED   CURRENT   ... CANARY
alpaca-prod         2         2         ... <none>
alpaca-test         1         1         ... true
bandicoot-prod      2         2         ... <none>
bandicoot-staging   1         1         ... <none>
```

You can remove a label by applying a dash suffix:

```
$ kubectl label deployments alpaca-test "canary-"
```

Label Selectors

Label selectors are used to filter Kubernetes objects based on a set of labels. Selectors use a simple Boolean language. They are used both by end users (via tools like kubectl) and by different types of objects (such as how ReplicaSet relates to its Pods).

Each deployment (via a ReplicaSet) creates a set of Pods using the labels specified in the template embedded in the deployment. This is configured by the `kubectl run` command.

Running the `kubectl get pods` command should return all the Pods currently running in the cluster. We should have a total of six kuard Pods across our three environments:

```
$ kubectl get pods --show-labels

NAME                           ... LABELS
alpaca-prod-3408831585-4nzfb   ... app=alpaca,env=prod,ver=1,...
alpaca-prod-3408831585-kgaθa   ... app=alpaca,env=prod,ver=1,...
alpaca-test-1004512375-3r1m5   ... app=alpaca,env=test,ver=2,...
bandicoot-prod-373860099-0t1gp ... app=bandicoot,env=prod,ver=2,...
bandicoot-prod-373860099-k2wcf ... app=bandicoot,env=prod,ver=2,...
bandicoot-staging-1839769971-3ndv ... app=bandicoot,env=staging,ver=2,...
```

You may see a new label that we haven't seen yet: `pod-template-hash`. This label is applied by the deployment so it can keep track of which pods were generated from which template versions. This allows the deployment to manage updates in a clean way, as will be covered in depth in Chapter 12.

If we only wanted to list pods that had the `ver` label set to 2 we could use the `--selector` flag:

```
$ kubectl get pods --selector="ver=2"

NAME                             READY   STATUS    RESTARTS   AGE
alpaca-test-1004512375-3r1m5     1/1     Running   0          3m
bandicoot-prod-373860099-0t1gp   1/1     Running   0          3m
bandicoot-prod-373860099-k2wcf   1/1     Running   0          3m
bandicoot-staging-1839769971-3ndv5 1/1   Running   0          3m
```

If we specify two selectors separated by a comma, only the objects that satisfy both will be returned. This is a logical AND operation:

```
$ kubectl get pods --selector="app=bandicoot,ver=2"

NAME                             READY   STATUS    RESTARTS   AGE
bandicoot-prod-373860099-0t1gp   1/1     Running   0          4m
bandicoot-prod-373860099-k2wcf   1/1     Running   0          4m
bandicoot-staging-1839769971-3ndv5 1/1   Running   0          4m
```

We can also ask if a label is one of a set of values. Here we ask for all pods where the app label is set to `alpaca` or `bandicoot` (which will be all six pods):

```
$ kubectl get pods --selector="app in (alpaca,bandicoot)"
```

```
NAME                             READY   STATUS    RESTARTS   AGE
alpaca-prod-3408831585-4nzfb     1/1     Running   0          6m
alpaca-prod-3408831585-kga0a     1/1     Running   0          6m
alpaca-test-1004512375-3r1m5     1/1     Running   0          6m
bandicoot-prod-373860099-0t1gp   1/1     Running   0          6m
bandicoot-prod-373860099-k2wcf   1/1     Running   0          6m
bandicoot-staging-1839769971-3ndv5  1/1  Running   0          6m
```

Finally, we can ask if a label is set at all. Here we are asking for all of the deployments with the canary label set to anything:

```
$ kubectl get deployments --selector="canary"
```

```
NAME         DESIRED   CURRENT   UP-TO-DATE   AVAILABLE   AGE
alpaca-test  1         1         1            1           7m
```

There are also "negative" versions of each of these, as shown in Table 6-2.

Table 6-2. Selector operators

Operator	Description
key=value	key is set to value
key!=value	key is not set to value
key in (value1, value2)	key is one of value1 or value2
key notin (value1, value2)	key is not one of value1 or value2
key	key is set
!key	key is not set

Label Selectors in API Objects

When a Kubernetes object refers to a set of other Kubernetes objects, a label selector is used. Instead of a simple string as described in the previous section, a parsed structure is used.

For historical reasons (Kubernetes doesn't break API compatibility!), there are two forms. Most objects support a newer, more powerful set of selector operators.

A selector of app=alpaca,ver in (1, 2) would be converted to this:

```
selector:
  matchLabels:
    app: alpaca
  matchExpressions:
    - {key: ver, operator: In, values: [1, 2]}  ❶
```

❶ Compact YAML syntax. This is an item in a list (matchExpressions) that is a map with three entries. The last entry (values) has a value that is a list with two items.

All of the terms are evaluated as a logical AND. The only way to represent the != operator is to convert it to a `NotIn` expression with a single value.

The older form of specifying selectors (used in `ReplicationControllers` and services) only supports the = operator. This is a simple set of key/value pairs that must all match a target object to be selected.

The selector `app=alpaca,ver=1` would be represented like this:

```
selector:
  app: alpaca
  ver: 1
```

Annotations

Annotations provide a place to store additional metadata for Kubernetes objects with the sole purpose of assisting tools and libraries. They are a way for other programs driving Kubernetes via an API to store some opaque data with an object. Annotations can be used for the tool itself or to pass configuration information between external systems.

While labels are used to identify and group objects, annotations are used to provide extra information about where an object came from, how to use it, or policy around that object. There is overlap, and it is a matter of taste as to when to use an annotation or a label. When in doubt, add information to an object as an annotation and promote it to a label if you find yourself wanting to use it in a selector.

Annotations are used to:

- Keep track of a "reason" for the latest update to an object.
- Communicate a specialized scheduling policy to a specialized scheduler.
- Extend data about the last tool to update the resource and how it was updated (used for detecting changes by other tools and doing a smart merge).
- Build, release, or image information that isn't appropriate for labels (may include a Git hash, timestamp, PR number, etc.).
- Enable the `Deployment` object (Chapter 12) to keep track of ReplicaSets that it is managing for rollouts.
- Provide extra data to enhance the visual quality or usability of a UI. For example, objects could include a link to an icon (or a base64-encoded version of an icon).
- Prototype alpha functionality in Kubernetes (instead of creating a first-class API field, the parameters for that functionality are instead encoded in an annotation).

Annotations are used in various places in Kubernetes, with the primary use case being rolling deployments. During rolling deployments, annotations are used to track rollout status and provide the necessary information required to roll back a deployment to a previous state.

Users should avoid using the Kubernetes API server as a general-purpose database. Annotations are good for small bits of data that are highly associated with a specific resource. If you want to store data in Kubernetes but you don't have an obvious object to associate it with, consider storing that data in some other, more appropriate database.

Defining Annotations

Annotation keys use the same format as label keys. However, because they are often used to communicate information between tools, the "namespace" part of the key is more important. Example keys include `deployment.kubernetes.io/revision` or `kubernetes.io/change-cause`.

The value component of an annotation is a free-form string field. While this allows maximum flexibility as users can store arbitrary data, because this is arbitrary text, there is no validation of any format. For example, it is not uncommon for a JSON document to be encoded as a string and stored in an annotation. It is important to note that the Kubernetes server has no knowledge of the required format of annotation values. If annotations are used to pass or store data, there is no guarantee the data is valid. This can make tracking down errors more difficult.

Annotations are defined in the common `metadata` section in every Kubernetes object:

```
...
metadata:
  annotations:
    example.com/icon-url: "https://example.com/icon.png"
...
```

Annotations are very convenient and provide powerful loose coupling. However, they should be used judiciously to avoid an untyped mess of data.

Cleanup

It is easy to clean up all of the deployments that we started in this chapter:

```
$ kubectl delete deployments --all
```

If you want to be more selective you can use the `--selector` flag to choose which deployments to delete.

Summary

Labels are used to identify and optionally group objects in a Kubernetes cluster. Labels are also used in selector queries to provide flexible runtime grouping of objects such as pods.

Annotations provide object-scoped key/value storage of metadata that can be used by automation tooling and client libraries. Annotations can also be used to hold configuration data for external tools such as third-party schedulers and monitoring tools.

Labels and annotations are key to understanding how key components in a Kubernetes cluster work together to ensure the desired cluster state. Using labels and annotations properly unlocks the true power of Kubernetes's flexibility and provides the starting point for building automation tools and deployment workflows.

## CHAPTER 7

Service Discovery

Kubernetes is a very dynamic system. The system is involved in placing Pods on nodes, making sure they are up and running, and rescheduling them as needed. There are ways to automatically change the number of pods based on load (such as horizontal pod autoscaling [see "Autoscaling a ReplicaSet" on page 84]). The API-driven nature of the system encourages others to create higher and higher levels of automation.

While the dynamic nature of Kubernetes makes it easy to run a lot of things, it creates problems when it comes to *finding* those things. Most of the traditional network infrastructure wasn't built for the level of dynamism that Kubernetes presents.

What Is Service Discovery?

The general name for this class of problems and solutions is *service discovery*. Service discovery tools help solve the problem of finding which processes are listening at which addresses for which services. A good service discovery system will enable users to resolve this information quickly and reliably. A good system is also low-latency; clients are updated soon after the information associated with a service changes. Finally, a good service discovery system can store a richer definition of what that service is. For example, perhaps there are multiple ports associated with the service.

The Domain Name System (DNS) is the traditional system of service discovery on the internet. DNS is designed for relatively stable name resolution with wide and efficient caching. It is a great system for the internet but falls short in the dynamic world of Kubernetes.

Unfortunately, many systems (for example, Java, by default) look up a name in DNS directly and never re-resolve. This can lead to clients caching stale mappings and talking to the wrong IP. Even with short TTLs and well-behaved clients, there is a natural delay between when a name resolution changes and the client notices. There are natural limits to the amount and type of information that can be returned in a typical DNS query, too. Things start to break past 20–30 A records for a single name. SRV records solve some problems but are often very hard to use. Finally, the way that clients handle multiple IPs in a DNS record is usually to take the first IP address and rely on the DNS server to randomize or round-robin the order of records. This is no substitute for more purpose-built load balancing.

The Service Object

Real service discovery in Kubernetes starts with a `Service` object.

A `Service object` is a way to create a named label selector. As we will see, the `Service` object does some other nice things for us too.

Just as the `kubectl run` command is an easy way to create a Kubernetes deployment, we can use `kubectl expose` to create a service. Let's create some deployments and services so we can see how they work:

```
$ kubectl run alpaca-prod \
  --image=gcr.io/kuar-demo/kuard-amd64:1 \
  --replicas=3 \
  --port=8080 \
  --labels="ver=1,app=alpaca,env=prod"
$ kubectl expose deployment alpaca-prod
$ kubectl run bandicoot-prod \
  --image=gcr.io/kuar-demo/kuard-amd64:2 \
  --replicas=2 \
  --port=8080 \
  --labels="ver=2,app=bandicoot,env=prod"
$ kubectl expose deployment bandicoot-prod
$ kubectl get services -o wide

NAME             CLUSTER-IP     ... PORT(S)  ... SELECTOR
alpaca-prod      10.115.245.13  ... 8080/TCP ... app=alpaca,env=prod,ver=1
bandicoot-prod   10.115.242.3   ... 8080/TCP ... app=bandicoot,env=prod,ver=2
kubernetes       10.115.240.1   ... 443/TCP  ... <none>
```

After running these commands, we have three services. The ones we just created are `alpaca-prod` and `bandicoot-prod`. The `kubernetes` service is automatically created for you so that you can find and talk to the Kubernetes API from within the app.

If we look at the `SELECTOR` column, we see that the `alpaca-prod` service simply gives a name to a selector and specifies which ports to talk to for that service. The `kubectl expose` command will conveniently pull both the label selector and the relevant ports (8080, in this case) from the deployment definition.

Furthermore, that service is assigned a new type of virtual IP called a *cluster IP*. This is a special IP address the system will load-balance across all of the pods that are identified by the selector.

To interact with services, we are going to port-forward to one of the `alpaca` pods. Start and leave this command running in a terminal window. You can see the port forward working by accessing the `alpaca` pod at *http://localhost:48858*:

```
$ ALPACA_POD=$(kubectl get pods -l app=alpaca \
    -o jsonpath='{.items[0].metadata.name}')
$ kubectl port-forward $ALPACA_POD 48858:8080
```

Service DNS

Because the cluster IP is virtual it is stable and it is appropriate to give it a DNS address. All of the issues around clients caching DNS results no longer apply. Within a namespace, it is as easy as just using the service name to connect to one of the pods identified by a service.

Kubernetes provides a DNS service exposed to Pods running in the cluster. This Kubernetes DNS service was installed as a system component when the cluster was first created. The DNS service is, itself, managed by Kubernetes and is a great example of Kubernetes building on Kubernetes. The Kubernetes DNS service provides DNS names for cluster IPs.

You can try this out by expanding the "DNS Resolver" section on the `kuard` server status page. Query the A record for `alpaca-prod`. The output should look something like this:

```
;; opcode: QUERY, status: NOERROR, id: 12071
;; flags: qr aa rd ra; QUERY: 1, ANSWER: 1, AUTHORITY: 0, ADDITIONAL: 0

;; QUESTION SECTION:
;alpaca-prod.default.svc.cluster.local. IN      A

;; ANSWER SECTION:
alpaca-prod.default.svc.cluster.local. 30     IN     A      10.115.245.13
```

The full DNS name here is `alpaca-prod.default.svc.cluster.local.`. Let's break this down:

`alpaca-prod`
    The name of the service in question.

`default`
    The namespace that this service is in.

svc:: *Recognizing that this is a service. This allows Kubernetes to expose other types of things as DNS in the future.* cluster.local.

The base domain name for the cluster. This is the default and what you will see for most clusters. Administrators may change this to allow unique DNS names across multiple clusters.

When referring to a service in your own namespace you can just use the service name (alpaca-prod). You can also refer to a service in another namespace with alpaca-prod.default. And, of course, you can use the fully qualified service name (alpaca-prod.default.svc.cluster.local.). Try each of these out in the "DNS Resolver" section of kuard.

Readiness Checks

Oftentimes when an application first starts up it isn't ready to handle requests. There is usually some amount of initialization that can take anywhere from under a second to several minutes. One nice thing the Service object does is track which of your pods are ready via a readiness check. Let's modify our deployment to add a readiness check:

```
$ kubectl edit deployment/alpaca-prod
```

This command will fetch the current version of the alpaca-prod deployment and bring it up in an editor. After you save and quit your editor, it'll then write the object back to Kubernetes. This is a quick way to edit an object without saving it to a YAML file.

Add the following section:

```
spec:
  ...
  template:
    ...
    spec:
      containers:
        ...
        name: alpaca-prod
        readinessProbe:
          httpGet:
            path: /ready
            port: 8080
          periodSeconds: 2
          initialDelaySeconds: 0
          failureThreshold: 3
          successThreshold: 1
```

This sets up the pods this deployment will create so that they will be checked for readiness via an HTTP GET to /ready on port 8080. This check is done every 2 seconds starting as soon as the pod comes up. If three successive checks fail, then the pod will be considered not ready. However, if only one check succeeds, then the pod will again be considered ready.

Only ready pods are sent traffic.

Updating the deployment definition like this will delete and recreate the `alpaca` pods. As such, we need to restart our `port-forward` command from earlier:

```
$ ALPACA_POD=$(kubectl get pods -l app=alpaca \
    -o jsonpath='{.items[0].metadata.name}')
$ kubectl port-forward $ALPACA_POD 48858:8080
```

Open your browser to *http://localhost:48858* and you should see the debug page for that instance of kuard. Expand the "Readiness Check" section. You should see this page update every time there is a new readiness check from the system, which should happen every 2 seconds.

In another terminal window, start a `watch` command on the endpoints for the `alpaca-prod` service. Endpoints are a lower-level way of finding what a service is sending traffic to and are covered later in this chapter. The `--watch` option here causes the `kubectl` command to hang around and output any updates. This is an easy way to see how a Kubernetes object changes over time:

```
$ kubectl get endpoints alpaca-prod --watch
```

Now go back to your browser and hit the "Fail" link for the readiness check. You should see that the server is not returning 500s. After three of these this server is removed from the list of endpoints for the service. Hit the "Succeed" link and notice that after a single readiness check the endpoint is added back.

This readiness check is a way for an overloaded or sick server to signal to the system that it doesn't want to receive traffic anymore. This is a great way to implement graceful shutdown. The server can signal that it no longer wants traffic, wait until existing connections are closed, and then cleanly exit.

Press Control-C to exit out of both the `port-forward` and `watch` commands in your terminals.

Looking Beyond the Cluster

So far, everything we've covered in this chapter has been about exposing services inside of a cluster. Oftentimes the IPs for pods are only reachable from within the cluster. At some point, we have to allow new traffic in!

The most portable way to do this is to use a feature called `NodePorts`, which enhance a service even further. In addition to a cluster IP, the system picks a port (or the user can specify one), and every node in the cluster then forwards traffic to that port to the service.

With this feature, if you can reach any node in the cluster you can contact a service. You use the `NodePort` without knowing where any of the Pods for that service are running. This can be integrated with hardware or software load balancers to expose the service further.

Try this out by modifying the `alpaca-prod` service:

```
$ kubectl edit service alpaca-prod
```

Change the `spec.type` field to `NodePort`. You can also do this when creating the service via kubectl `expose` by specifying `--type=NodePort`. The system will assign a new `NodePort`:

```
$ kubectl describe service alpaca-prod
```

```
Name:               alpaca-prod
Namespace:          default
Labels:             app=alpaca
                    env=prod
                    ver=1
Annotations:        <none>
Selector:           app=alpaca,env=prod,ver=1
Type:               NodePort
IP:                 10.115.245.13
Port:               <unset> 8080/TCP
NodePort:           <unset> 32711/TCP
Endpoints:          10.112.1.66:8080,10.112.2.104:8080,10.112.2.105:8080
Session Affinity:   None
No events.
```

Here we see that the system assigned port 32711 to this service. Now we can hit any of our cluster nodes on that port to access the service. If you are sitting on the same network, you can access it directly. If your cluster is in the cloud someplace, you can use SSH tunneling with something like this:

```
$ ssh <node> -L 8080:localhost:32711
```

Now if you open your browser to *http://localhost:8080* you will be connected to that service. Each request that you send to the service will be randomly directed to one of the Pods that implement the service. Reload the page a few times and you will see that you are randomly assigned to different pods.

When you are done, exit out of the SSH session.

Cloud Integration

Finally, if you have support from the cloud that you are running on (and your cluster is configured to take advantage of it) you can use the `LoadBalancer` type. This builds on `NodePorts` by additionally configuring the cloud to create a new load balancer and direct it at nodes in your cluster.

Edit the `alpaca-prod` service again (kubectl edit service alpaca-prod) and change `spec.type` to `LoadBalancer`.

If you do a `kubectl get services` right away you'll see that the `EXTERNAL-IP` column for `alpaca-prod` now says `<pending>`. Wait a bit and you should see a public address assigned by your cloud. You can look in the console for your cloud account and see the configuration work that Kubernetes did for you:

```
$ kubectl describe service alpaca-prod

Name:                   alpaca-prod
Namespace:              default
Labels:                 app=alpaca
                        env=prod
                        ver=1
Selector:               app=alpaca,env=prod,ver=1
Type:                   LoadBalancer
IP:                     10.115.245.13
LoadBalancer Ingress:   104.196.248.204
Port:                   <unset> 8080/TCP
NodePort:               <unset> 32711/TCP
Endpoints:              10.112.1.66:8080,10.112.2.104:8080,10.112.2.105:8080
Session Affinity:       None
Events:
  FirstSeen ... Reason                  Message
  --------- ... ------                  -------
  3m        ... Type                    NodePort -> LoadBalancer
  3m        ... CreatingLoadBalancer    Creating load balancer
  2m        ... CreatedLoadBalancer     Created load balancer
```

Here we see that we have an address of 104.196.248.204 now assigned to the `alpaca-prod` service. Open up your browser and try!

This example is from a cluster launched and managed on the Google Cloud Platform via GKE. However, the way a `LoadBalancer` is configured is specific to a cloud. In addition, some clouds have DNS-based load balancers (e.g., AWS ELB). In this case you'll see a hostname here instead of an IP. Also, depending on the cloud provider, it may still take a little while for the load balancer to be fully operational.

Advanced Details

Kubernetes is built to be an extensible system. As such, there are layers that allow for more advanced integrations. Understanding the details of how a sophisticated concept like services is implemented may help you troubleshoot or create more advanced integrations. This section goes a bit below the surface.

Endpoints

Some applications (and the system itself) want to be able to use services without using a cluster IP. This is done with another type of object called `Endpoints`. For every `Service` object, Kubernetes creates a buddy `Endpoints` object that contains the IP addresses for that service:

```
$ kubectl describe endpoints alpaca-prod

Name:               alpaca-prod
Namespace:          default
Labels:             app=alpaca
                    env=prod
                    ver=1
Subsets:
  Addresses:              10.112.1.54,10.112.2.84,10.112.2.85
  NotReadyAddresses:      <none>
  Ports:
    Name      Port    Protocol
    ----      ----    --------
    <unset>   8080    TCP

No events.
```

To use a service, an advanced application can talk to the Kubernetes API directly to look up endpoints and call them. The Kubernetes API even has the capability to "watch" objects and be notified as soon as they change. In this way a client can react immediately as soon as the IPs associated with a service change.

Let's demonstrate this. In a terminal window, start the following command and leave it running:

```
$ kubectl get endpoints alpaca-prod --watch
```

It will output the current state of the endpoint and then "hang":

```
NAME          ENDPOINTS                                                 AGE
alpaca-prod   10.112.1.54:8080,10.112.2.84:8080,10.112.2.85:8080        1m
```

Now open up *another* terminal window and delete and recreate the deployment backing alpaca-prod:

```
$ kubectl delete deployment alpaca-prod
$ kubectl run alpaca-prod \
  --image=gcr.io/kuar-demo/kuard-amd64:1 \
  --replicas=3 \
  --port=8080 \
  --labels="ver=1,app=alpaca,env=prod"
```

If you look back at the output from the watched endpoint, you will see that as you deleted and re-created these pods, the output of the command reflected the most up-to-date set of IP addresses associated with the service. Your output will look something like this:

```
NAME          ENDPOINTS                                              AGE
alpaca-prod   10.112.1.54:8080,10.112.2.84:8080,10.112.2.85:8080     1m
alpaca-prod   10.112.1.54:8080,10.112.2.84:8080     1m
alpaca-prod   <none>    1m
alpaca-prod   10.112.2.90:8080    1m
alpaca-prod   10.112.1.57:8080,10.112.2.90:8080     1m
alpaca-prod   10.112.0.28:8080,10.112.1.57:8080,10.112.2.90:8080     1m
```

The Endpoints object is great if you are writing new code that is built to run on Kubernetes from the start. But most projects aren't in this position! Most existing systems are built to work with regular old IP addresses that don't change that often.

Manual Service Discovery

Kubernetes services are built on top of label selectors over pods. That means that you can use the Kubernetes API to do rudimentary service discovery without using a Service object at all! Let's demonstrate.

With kubectl (and via the API) we can easily see what IPs are assigned to each pod in our example deployments:

```
$ kubectl get pods -o wide --show-labels

NAME                        ... IP            ... LABELS
alpaca-prod-12334-87f8h     ... 10.112.1.54 ... app=alpaca,env=prod,ver=1
alpaca-prod-12334-jssmh     ... 10.112.2.84 ... app=alpaca,env=prod,ver=1
alpaca-prod-12334-tjp56     ... 10.112.2.85 ... app=alpaca,env=prod,ver=1
bandicoot-prod-5678-sbxzl   ... 10.112.1.55 ... app=bandicoot,env=prod,ver=2
bandicoot-prod-5678-x0dh8   ... 10.112.2.86 ... app=bandicoot,env=prod,ver=2
```

This is great, but what if you have a ton of pods? You'll probably want to filter this based on the labels applied as part of the deployment. Let's do that for just the alpaca app:

```
$ kubectl get pods -o wide --selector=app=alpaca,env=prod

NAME                          ... IP          ...
alpaca-prod-3408831585-bpzdz ... 10.112.1.54 ...
alpaca-prod-3408831585-kncwt ... 10.112.2.84 ...
alpaca-prod-3408831585-l9fsq ... 10.112.2.85 ...
```

At this point we have the basics of service discovery! We can always use labels to identify the set of pods we are interested in, get all of the pods for those labels, and dig out the IP address. But keeping the correct set of labels to use in sync can be tricky. This is why the Service object was created.

kube-proxy and Cluster IPs

Cluster IPs are stable virtual IPs that load-balance traffic across all of the endpoints in a service. This magic is performed by a component running on every node in the cluster called the kube-proxy (Figure 7-1).

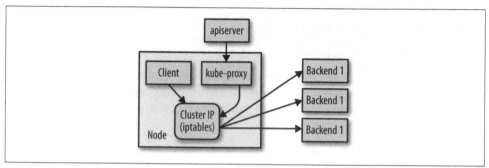

Figure 7-1. Configuring and using a cluster IP

In Figure 7-1, the kube-proxy watches for new services in the cluster via the API server. It then programs a set of iptables rules in the kernel of that host to rewrite the destination of packets so they are directed at one of the endpoints for that service. If the set of endpoints for a service changes (due to pods coming and going or due to a failed readiness check) the set of iptables rules is rewritten.

The cluster IP itself is usually assigned by the API server as the service is created. However, when creating the service, the user can specify a specific cluster IP. Once set, the cluster IP cannot be modified without deleting and recreating the Service object.

The Kubernetes service address range is configured using the --service-cluster-ip-range flag on the kube-apiserver binary. The service address range should not overlap with the IP subnets and ranges assigned to each Docker bridge or Kubernetes node.

In addition, any explicit cluster IP requested must come from that range and not already be in use.

Cluster IP Environment Variables

While most users should be using the DNS services to find cluster IPs, there are some older mechanisms that may still be in use. One of these is injecting a set of environment variables into pods as they start up.

To see this in action, let's look at the console for the bandicoot instance of kuard. Enter the following commands in your terminal:

```
$ BANDICOOT_POD=$(kubectl get pods -l app=bandicoot \
    -o jsonpath='{.items[0].metadata.name}')
$ kubectl port-forward $BANDICOOT_POD 48858:8080
```

Now open your browser to *http://localhost:48858* to see the status page for this server. Expand the "Environment" section and note the set of environment variables for the alpaca service. The status page should show a table similar to Table 7-1.

Table 7-1. Service environment variables

Name	Value
ALPACA_PROD_PORT	tcp://10.115.245.13:8080
ALPACA_PROD_PORT_0000_TCP	tcp://10.115.245.13:8080
ALPACA_PROD_PORT_8080_TCP_ADDR	10.115.245.13
ALPACA_PROD_PORT_8080_TCP_PORT	8080
ALPACA_PROD_PORT_8080_TCP_PROTO	tcp
ALPACA_PROD_SERVICE_HOST	10.115.245.13
ALPACA_PROD_SERVICE_PORT	8080

The two main environment variables to use are ALPACA_PROD_SERVICE_HOST and ALPACA_PROD_SERVICE_PORT. The other environment variables are created to be compatible with (now deprecated) Docker link variables.

A problem with the environment variable approach is that it requires resources to be created in a specific order. The services must be created before the pods that reference them. This can introduce quite a bit of complexity when deploying a set of services that make up a larger application. In addition, using *just* environment variables seems strange to many users. For this reason, DNS is probably a better option.

Cleanup

Run the following commands to clean up all of the objects created in this chapter:

```
$ kubectl delete services,deployments -l app
```

Summary

Kubernetes is a dynamic system that challenges traditional methods of naming and connecting services over the network. The Service object provides a flexible and powerful way to expose services both within the cluster and beyond. With the techniques covered here you can connect services to each other and expose them outside the cluster.

While using the dynamic service discovery mechanisms in Kubernetes introduces some new concepts and may, at first, seem complex, understanding and adapting these techniques is key to unlocking the power of Kubernetes. Once your application can dynamically find services and react to the dynamic placement of those applications, you are free to stop worrying about where things are running and when they move. It is a critical piece of the puzzle to start to think about services in a logical way and let Kubernetes take care of the details of container placement.

## CHAPTER 8

ReplicaSets

Previously, we covered how to run individual containers as Pods. But these pods are essentially one-off singletons. More often than not, you want multiple replicas of a container running at a particular time. There are a variety of reasons for this type of replication:

Redundancy
 Multiple running instances mean failure can be tolerated.

Scale
 Multiple running instances mean that more requests can be handled.

Sharding
 Different replicas can handle different parts of a computation in parallel.

Of course, you could manually create multiple copies of a Pod using multiple different (though largely similar) Pod manifests, but doing so is both tedious and error-prone. Logically, a user managing a replicated set of Pods considers them as a single entity to be defined and managed. This is precisely what a ReplicaSet is. A ReplicaSet acts as a cluster-wide Pod manager, ensuring that the right types and number of Pods are running at all times.

Because ReplicaSets make it easy to create and manage replicated sets of Pods, they are the building blocks used to describe common application deployment patterns and provide the underpinnings of self-healing for our applications at the infrastructure level. Pods managed by ReplicaSets are automatically rescheduled under certain failure conditions such as node failures and network partitions.

The easiest way to think of a ReplicaSet is that it combines a cookie cutter and a desired of number of cookies into a single API object. When we define a ReplicaSet, we define a specification for the Pods we want to create (the "cookie cutter"), and a desired number of replicas. Additionally, we need to define a way of finding Pods that the ReplicaSet should control. The actual act of managing the replicated Pods is an example of a *reconciliation loop*. Such loops are fundamental to most of the design and implementation of Kubernetes.

Reconciliation Loops

The central concept behind a reconciliation loop is the notion of *desired* state and *observed* or *current* state. Desired state is the state you want. With a ReplicaSet it is the desired number of replicas and the definition of the Pod to replicate. For example, the desired state is that there are three replicas of a Pod running the kuard server.

In contrast, current state is the currently observed state of the system. For example, there are only two kuard Pods currently running.

The reconciliation loop is constantly running, observing the current state of the world and taking action to try to make the observed state match the desired state. For example, given the previous example, the reconciliation loop creates a new kuard Pod in an effort to make the observed state match the desired state of three replicas.

There are many benefits to the reconciliation loop approach to managing state. It is an inherently goal-driven, self-healing system, yet it can often be easily expressed in a few lines of code.

As a concrete example of this, note that the reconciliation loop for ReplicaSets is a single loop, and yet it handles both user actions to scale up or scale down the Replica-Set, as well as node failures or nodes rejoining the cluster after being absent.

Throughout the rest of the book we'll see numerous examples of reconciliation loops in action.

Relating Pods and ReplicaSets

One of the key themes that runs through Kubernetes is decoupling. In particular, it's important that all of the core concepts of Kubernetes are modular with respect to each other and that they are swappable and replaceable with other components. In this spirit, the relationship between ReplicaSets and Pods is loosely coupled. Though ReplicaSets create and manage Pods, they do not own the Pods they create. Replica-Sets use label queries to identify the set of Pods they should be managing. They then use the exact same Pod API that you used directly in Chapter 5 to create the Pods that they are managing. This notion of "coming in the front door" is another central design concept in Kubernetes. In a similar decoupling, ReplicaSets that create multiple Pods and the services that load-balance to those Pods are also totally separate, decoupled API objects. In addition to supporting modularity, the decoupling of Pods and ReplicaSets enables several important behaviors, discussed in the following sections.

Adopting Existing Containers

Despite the value placed on declarative configuration of software, there are times when it is easier to build something up imperatively. In particular, early on you may be simply deploying a single Pod with a container image without a ReplicaSet managing it. But at some point you may want to expand your singleton container into a replicated service and create and manage an array of similar containers. You may have even defined a load balancer that is serving traffic to that single Pod. If Replica-Sets owned the Pods they created, then the only way to start replicating your Pod would be to delete it and then relaunch it via a ReplicaSet. This might be disruptive, as there would be a moment in time when there would be no copies of your container running. However, because ReplicaSets are decoupled from the Pods they manage, you can simply create a ReplicaSet that will "adopt" the existing Pod, and scale out additional copies of those containers. In this way you can seamlessly move from a single imperative Pod to a replicated set of Pods managed by a ReplicaSet.

Quarantining Containers

Oftentimes, when a server misbehaves, Pod-level health checks will automatically restart that Pod. But if your health checks are incomplete, a Pod can be misbehaving but still be part of the replicated set. In these situations, while it would work to simply kill the Pod, that would leave your developers with only logs to debug the problem. Instead, you can modify the set of labels on the sick Pod. Doing so will disassociate it from the ReplicaSet (and service) so that you can debug the Pod. The ReplicaSet controller will notice that a Pod is missing and create a new copy, but because the Pod is still running, it is available to developers for interactive debugging, which is significantly more valuable than debugging from logs.

Designing with ReplicaSets

ReplicaSets are designed to represent a single, scalable microservice inside your architecture. The key characteristic of ReplicaSets is that every Pod that is created by the ReplicaSet controller is entirely homogeneous. Typically, these Pods are then fronted by a Kubernetes service load balancer, which spreads traffic across the Pods that make up the service. Generally speaking, ReplicaSets are designed for stateles (or nearly stateless) services. The elements created by the ReplicaSet are interchangeable; when a ReplicaSet is scaled down, an arbitrary Pod is selected for deletion. Your application's behavior shouldn't change because of such a scale-down operation.

ReplicaSet Spec

Like all concepts in Kubernetes, ReplicaSets are defined using a specification. All ReplicaSets must have a unique name (defined using the `metadata.name` field), a `spec` section that describes the number of Pods (replicas) that should be running cluster-wide at a given time, and a Pod template that describes the Pod to be created when the defined number of replicas is not met. Example 8-1 shows a minimal ReplicaSet definition.

Example 8-1. kuard-rs.yaml

```
apiVersion: extensions/v1beta1
kind: ReplicaSet
metadata:
  name: kuard
spec:
  replicas: 1
  template:
    metadata:
      labels:
        app: kuard
        version: "2"
    spec:
      containers:
        - name: kuard
          image: "gcr.io/kuar-demo/kuard-amd64:2"
```

Pod Templates

As mentioned previously, when the number of Pods in the current state is less than the number of Pods in the desired state, the ReplicaSet controller will create new Pods. The Pods are created using a Pod template that is contained in the ReplicaSet specification. The Pods are created in exactly the same manner as when you created a Pod from a YAML file in previous chapters. But instead of using a file, the Kubernetes ReplicaSet controller creates and submits a Pod manifest based on the Pod template directly to the API server. The following shows an example of a Pod template in a ReplicaSet:

```
template:
  metadata:
    labels:
      app: helloworld
      version: v1
  spec:
    containers:
      - name: helloworld
        image: kelseyhightower/helloworld:v1
```

```
    ports:
      - containerPort: 80
```

Labels

In any cluster of reasonable size, there are many different Pods running at any given time—so how does the ReplicaSet reconciliation loop discover the set of Pods for a particular ReplicaSet? ReplicaSets monitor cluster state using a set of Pod labels. Labels are used to filter Pod listings and track Pods running within a cluster. When ReplicaSets are initially created, the ReplicaSet fetches a Pod listing from the Kubernetes API and filters the results by labels. Based on the number of Pods returned by the query, the ReplicaSet deletes or creates Pods to meet the desired number of replicas. The labels used for filtering are defined in the ReplicaSet spec section and are the key to understanding how ReplicaSets work.

 The selector in the ReplicaSet spec should be a proper subset of the labels in the Pod template.

Creating a ReplicaSet

ReplicaSets are created by submitting a ReplicaSet object to the Kubernetes API. In this section we will create a ReplicaSet using a configuration file and the kubectl apply command.

The ReplicaSet configuration file in Example 8-1 will ensure one copy of the gcr.io/kuar-demo/kuard-amd64:1 container is running at a given time.

Use the kubectl apply command to submit the kuard ReplicaSet to the Kubernetes API:

```
$ kubectl apply -f kuard-rs.yaml
replicaset "kuard" created
```

Once the kuard ReplicaSet has been accepted, the ReplicaSet controller will detect there are no kuard Pods running that match the desired state, and a new kuard Pod will be created based on the contents of the Pod template:

```
$ kubectl get pods
NAME          READY   STATUS    RESTARTS   AGE
kuard-yvzgd   1/1     Running   0          11s
```

Inspecting a ReplicaSet

As with Pods and other Kubernetes API objects, if you are interested in further details about a ReplicaSet, the describe command will provide much more information about its state. Here is an example of using describe to obtain the details of the ReplicaSet we previously created:

```
$ kubectl describe rs kuard
Name:          kuard
Namespace:     default
Image(s):      kuard:1.9.15
Selector:      app=kuard,version=2
Labels:        app=kuard,version=2
Replicas:      1 current / 1 desired
Pods Status:   1 Running / 0 Waiting / 0 Succeeded / 0 Failed
No volumes.
```

You can see the label selector for the ReplicaSet, as well as the state of all of the replicas managed by the ReplicaSet.

Finding a ReplicaSet from a Pod

Sometimes you may wonder if a Pod is being managed by a ReplicaSet, and, if it is, which ReplicaSet.

To enable this kind of discovery, the ReplicaSet controller adds an annotation to every Pod that it creates. The key for the annotation is kubernetes.io/created-by. If you run the following, look for the kubernetes.io/created-by entry in the annotations section:

```
$ kubectl get pods <pod-name> -o yaml
```

If applicable, this will list the name of the ReplicaSet that is managing this Pod. Note that such annotations are best-effort; they are only created when the Pod is created by the ReplicaSet, and can be removed by a Kubernetes user at any time.

Finding a Set of Pods for a ReplicaSet

You can also determine the set of Pods managed by a ReplicaSet. First, you can get the set of labels using the kubectl describe command. In the previous example, the label selector was app=kuard,version=2. To find the Pods that match this selector, use the --selector flag or the shorthand -l:

```
$ kubectl get pods -l app=kuard,version=2
```

This is exactly the same query that the ReplicaSet executes to determine the current number of Pods.

Scaling ReplicaSets

ReplicaSets are scaled up or down by updating the `spec.replicas` key on the ReplicaSet object stored in Kubernetes. When a ReplicaSet is scaled up, new Pods are submitted to the Kubernetes API using the Pod template defined on the ReplicaSet.

Imperative Scaling with kubectl Scale

The easiest way to achieve this is using the `scale` command in `kubectl`. For example, to scale up to four replicas you could run:

```
$ kubectl scale kuard --replicas=4
```

While such imperative commands are useful for demonstrations and quick reactions to emergency situations (e.g., in response to a sudden increase in load), it is important to also update any text-file configurations to match the number of replicas that you set via the imperative `scale` command. The reason for this becomes obvious when you consider the following scenario:

> Alice is on call, when suddenly there is a large increase in load on the service she is managing. Alice uses the +scale+ command to increase the number of servers responding to requests to 10, and the situation is resolved. However, Alice forgets to update the ReplicaSet configurations checked into source control. Several days later, Bob is preparing the weekly rollouts. Bob edits the ReplicaSet configurations stored in version control to use the new container image, but he doesn't notice that the number of replicas in the file is currently 5, not the 10 that Alice set in response to the increased load. Bob proceeds with the rollout, which both updates the container image and reduces the number of replicas by half, causing an immediate overload or outage.

Hopefully, this illustrates the need to ensure that any imperative changes are immediately followed by a declarative change in source control. Indeed, if the need is not acute, we generally recommend only making declarative changes as described in the following section.

Declaratively Scaling with kubectl apply

In a declarative world, we make changes by editing the configuration file in version control and then applying those changes to our cluster. To scale the `kuard` ReplicaSet, edit the *kuard-rs.yaml* configuration file and set the `replicas` count to 3:

```
...
spec:
  replicas: 3
...
```

In a multiuser setting, you would like to have a documented code review of this change and eventually check the changes into version control. Either way, you can then use the kubectl apply command to submit the updated kuard ReplicaSet to the API server:

```
$ kubectl apply -f kuard-rs.yaml
replicaset "kuard" configured
```

Now that the updated kuard ReplicaSet is in place, the ReplicaSet controller will detect that the number of desired Pods has changed and that it needs to take action to realize that desired state. If you used the imperative scale command in the previous section, the ReplicaSet controller will destroy one Pod to get the number to three. Otherwise, it will submit two new Pods to the Kubernetes API using the Pod template defined on the kuard ReplicaSet. Regardless, use the kubectl get pods command to list the running kuard Pods. You should see output like the following:

```
$ kubectl get pods
NAME          READY   STATUS    RESTARTS   AGE
kuard-3a2sb   1/1     Running   0          26s
kuard-wuq9v   1/1     Running   0          26s
kuard-yvzgd   1/1     Running   0          2m
```

Autoscaling a ReplicaSet

While there will be times when you want to have explicit control over the number of replicas in a ReplicaSet, often you simply want to have "enough" replicas. The definition varies depending on the needs of the containers in the ReplicaSet. For example, with a web server like nginx, you may want to scale due to CPU usage. For an in-memory cache, you may want to scale with memory consumption. In some cases you may want to scale in response to custom application metrics. Kubernetes can handle all of these scenarios via *horizontal pod autoscaling* (HPA).

HPA requires the presence of the heapster Pod on your cluster. heapster keeps track of metrics and provides an API for consuming metrics HPA uses when making scaling decisions. Most installations of Kubernetes include heapster by default. You can validate its presence by listing the Pods in the kube-system namespace:

```
$ kubectl get pods --namespace=kube-system
```

You should see a Pod named heapster somewhere in that list. If you do not see it, autoscaling will not work correctly.

"Horizontal pod autoscaling" is kind of a mouthful, and you might wonder why it is not simply called "autoscaling." Kubernetes makes a distinction between *horizontal* scaling, which involves creating additional replicas of a Pod, and *vertical* scaling, which involves increasing the resources required for a particular Pod (e.g., increasing the CPU required for the Pod). Vertical scaling is not currently implemented in Kubernetes, but it is planned. Additionally, many solutions also enable *cluster* autoscaling, where the number of machines in the cluster is scaled in response to resource needs, but this solution is not covered here.

Autoscaling based on CPU

Scaling based on CPU usage is the most common use case for Pod autoscaling. Generally it is most useful for request-based systems that consume CPU proportionally to the number of requests they are receiving, while using a relatively static amount of memory.

To scale a ReplicaSet, you can run a command like the following:

```
$ kubectl autoscale rs kuard --min=2 --max=5 --cpu-percent=80
```

This command creates an autoscaler that scales between two and five replicas with a CPU threshold of 80%. To view, modify, or delete this resource you can use the standard kubectl commands and the `horizontalpodautoscalers` resource. `horizontalpodautoscalers` is quite a bit to type, but it can be shortened to hpa:

```
$ kubectl get hpa
```

> Because of the decoupled nature of Kubernetes, there is no direct link between the horizontal pod autoscaler and the ReplicaSet. While this is great for modularity and composition, it also enables some antipatterns. In particular, it's a bad idea to combine both autoscaling and imperative or declarative management of the number of replicas. If both you and an autoscaler are attempting to modify the number of replicas, it's highly likely that you will clash, resulting in unexpected behavior.

Deleting ReplicaSets

When a ReplicaSet set is no longer required it can be deleted using the kubectl delete command. By default, this also deletes the Pods that are managed by the ReplicaSet:

```
$ kubectl delete rs kuard
replicaset "kuard" deleted
```

Running the kubectl get pods command shows that all the kuard Pods created by the kuard ReplicaSet have also been deleted:

```
$ kubectl get pods
```

If you don't want to delete the Pods that are being managed by the ReplicaSet you can set the --cascade flag to false to ensure only the ReplicaSet object is deleted and not the Pods:

```
$ kubectl delete rs kuard --cascade=false
```

Summary

Composing Pods with ReplicaSets provides the foundation for building robust applications with automatic failover, and makes deploying those applications a breeze by enabling scalable and sane deployment patterns. ReplicaSets should be used for any Pod you care about, even if it is a single Pod! Some people even default to using ReplicaSets instead of Pods. A typical cluster will have many ReplicaSets, so apply liberally to the affected area.

## CHAPTER 9

DaemonSets

ReplicaSets are generally about creating a service (e.g., a web server) with multiple replicas for redundancy. But that is not the only reason you may want to replicate a set of Pods within a cluster. Another reason to replicate a set of Pods is to schedule a single Pod on every node within the cluster. Generally, the motivation for replicating a Pod to every node is to land some sort of agent or daemon on each node, and the Kubernetes object for achieving this is the DaemonSet.

A DaemonSet ensures a copy of a Pod is running across a set of nodes in a Kubernetes cluster. DaemonSets are used to deploy system daemons such as log collectors and monitoring agents, which typically must run on every node. DaemonSets share similar functionality with ReplicaSets; both create Pods that are expected to be long-running services and ensure that the desired state and the observed state of the cluster match.

Given the similarities between DaemonSets and ReplicaSets, it's important to understand when to use one over the other. ReplicaSets should be used when your application is completely decoupled from the node and you can run multiple copies on a given node without special consideration. DaemonSets should be used when a single copy of your application must run on all or a subset of the nodes in the cluster.

You should generally not use scheduling restrictions or other parameters to ensure that Pods do not colocate on the same node. If you find yourself wanting a single Pod per node, then a DaemonSet is the correct Kubernetes resource to use. Likewise, if you find yourself building a homogeneous replicated service to serve user traffic, then a ReplicaSet is probably the right Kubernetes resource to use.

DaemonSet Scheduler

By default a DaemonSet will create a copy of a Pod on every node unless a node selector is used, which will limit eligible nodes to those with a matching set of labels. DaemonSets determine which node a Pod will run on at Pod creation time by specifying the nodeName field in the Pod spec. As a result, Pods created by DaemonSets are ignored by the Kubernetes scheduler.

Like ReplicaSets, DaemonSets are managed by a reconciliation control loop that measures the desired state (a Pod is present on all nodes) with the observed state (is the Pod present on a particular node?). Given this information, the DaemonSet controller creates a Pod on each node that doesn't currently have a matching Pod.

If a new node is added to the cluster, then the DaemonSet controller notices that it is missing a Pod and adds the Pod to the new node.

> DaemonSets and ReplicaSets are a great demonstration of the value of Kubernetes's decoupled architecture. It might seem that the right design would be for a ReplicaSet to own the Pods it manages, and for Pods to be subresources of a ReplicaSet. Likewise, the Pods managed by a DaemonSet would be subresources of that DaemonSet. However, this kind of encapsulation would require that tools for dealing with Pods be written two different times, one for DaemonSets and one for ReplicaSets. Instead, Kubernetes uses a decoupled approach where Pods are top-level objects. This means that every tool you have learned for introspecting Pods in the context of ReplicaSets (e.g., kubectl logs *<pod-name>*) is equally applicable to Pods created by DaemonSets.

Creating DaemonSets

DaemonSets are created by submitting a DaemonSet configuration to the Kubernetes API server. The following DaemonSet will create a fluentd logging agent on every node in the target cluster (Example 9-1).

Example 9-1. fluentd.yaml

```
apiVersion: extensions/v1beta1
kind: DaemonSet
metadata:
  name: fluentd
  namespace: kube-system
  labels:
    app: fluentd
spec:
  template:
```

```
metadata:
  labels:
    app: fluentd
spec:
  containers:
  - name: fluentd
    image: fluent/fluentd:v0.14.10
    resources:
      limits:
        memory: 200Mi
      requests:
        cpu: 100m
        memory: 200Mi
    volumeMounts:
    - name: varlog
      mountPath: /var/log
    - name: varlibdockercontainers
      mountPath: /var/lib/docker/containers
      readOnly: true
  terminationGracePeriodSeconds: 30
  volumes:
  - name: varlog
    hostPath:
      path: /var/log
  - name: varlibdockercontainers
    hostPath:
      path: /var/lib/docker/containers
```

DaemonSets require a unique name across all DaemonSets in a given Kubernetes namespace. Each DaemonSet must include a Pod template spec, which will be used to create Pods as needed. This is where the similarities between ReplicaSets and DaemonSets end. Unlike ReplicaSets, DaemonSets will create Pods on every node in the cluster by default unless a node selector is used.

Once you have a valid DaemonSet configuration in place, you can use the kubectl apply command to submit the DaemonSet to the Kubernetes API. In this section we will create a DaemonSet to ensure the fluentd HTTP server is running on every node in our cluster:

```
$ kubectl apply -f fluentd.yaml
daemonset "fluentd" created
```

Once the fluentd DaemonSet has been successfully submitted to the Kubernetes API, you can query its current state using the kubectl describe command:

```
$ kubectl describe daemonset fluentd
Name:           fluentd
Image(s):       fluent/fluentd:v0.14.10
Selector:       app=fluentd
Node-Selector:  <none>
Labels:         app=fluentd
```

```
Desired Number of Nodes Scheduled: 3
Current Number of Nodes Scheduled: 3
Number of Nodes Misscheduled: 0
Pods Status:    3 Running / 0 Waiting / 0 Succeeded / 0 Failed
```

This output indicates a `fluentd` Pod was successfully deployed to all three nodes in our cluster. We can verify this using the `kubectl get pods` command with the `-o` flag to print the nodes where each fluentd Pod was assigned:

```
$ kubectl get pods -o wide

NAME            AGE    NODE
fluentd-1q6c6   13m    k0-default-pool-35609c18-z7tb
fluentd-mwi7h   13m    k0-default-pool-35609c18-ydae
fluentd-zr6l7   13m    k0-default-pool-35609c18-pol3
```

With the `fluentd` DaemonSet in place, adding a new node to the cluster will result in a `fluentd` Pod being deployed to that node automatically:

```
$ kubectl get pods -o wide
NAME            AGE    NODE
fluentd-1q6c6   13m    k0-default-pool-35609c18-z7tb
fluentd-mwi7h   13m    k0-default-pool-35609c18-ydae
fluentd-oipmq   43s    k0-default-pool-35609c18-0xnl
fluentd-zr6l7   13m    k0-default-pool-35609c18-pol3
```

This is exactly the behavior you want when managing logging daemons and other cluster-wide services. No action was required from our end; this is how the Kubernetes DaemonSet controller reconciles its observed state with our desired state.

Limiting DaemonSets to Specific Nodes

The most common use case for DaemonSets is to run a Pod across every node in a Kubernetes cluster. However, there are some cases where you want to deploy a Pod to only a subset of nodes. For example, maybe you have a workload that requires a GPU or access to fast storage only available on a subset of nodes in your cluster. In cases like these node labels can be used to tag specific nodes that meet workload requirements.

Adding Labels to Nodes

The first step in limiting DaemonSets to specific nodes is to add the desired set of labels to a subset of nodes. This can be achieved using the `kubectl label` command.

The following command adds the `ssd=true` label to a single node:

```
$ kubectl label nodes k0-default-pool-35609c18-z7tb ssd=true
node "k0-default-pool-35609c18-z7tb" labeled
```

Just like with other Kubernetes resources, listing nodes without a label selector returns all nodes in the cluster:

```
$ kubectl get nodes
NAME                             STATUS   AGE
k0-default-pool-35609c18-0xnl    Ready    23m
k0-default-pool-35609c18-pol3    Ready    1d
k0-default-pool-35609c18-ydae    Ready    1d
k0-default-pool-35609c18-z7tb    Ready    1d
```

Using a label selector we can filter nodes based on labels. To list only the nodes that have the ssd label set to true, use the kubectl get nodes command with the --selector flag:

```
$ kubectl get nodes --selector ssd=true
NAME                             STATUS   AGE
k0-default-pool-35609c18-z7tb    Ready    1d
```

Node Selectors

Node selectors can be used to limit what nodes a Pod can run on in a given Kubernetes cluster. Node selectors are defined as part of the Pod spec when creating a DaemonSet. The following DaemonSet configuration limits nginx to running only on nodes with the ssd=true label set (Example 9-2).

Example 9-2. nginx-fast-storage.yaml

```
apiVersion: extensions/v1beta1
kind: "DaemonSet"
metadata:
  labels:
    app: nginx
    ssd: "true"
  name: nginx-fast-storage
spec:
  template:
    metadata:
      labels:
        app: nginx
        ssd: "true"
    spec:
      nodeSelector:
        ssd: "true"
      containers:
        - name: nginx
          image: nginx:1.10.0
```

Let's see what happens when we submit the nginx-fast-storage DaemonSet to the Kubernetes API:

```
$ kubectl apply -f nginx-fast-storage.yaml
daemonset "nginx-fast-storage" created
```

Since there is only one node with the `ssd=true` label, the `nginx-fast-storage` Pod will only run on that node:

```
$ kubectl get pods -o wide
NAME                         STATUS    NODE
nginx-fast-storage-7b90t     Running   k0-default-pool-35609c18-z7tb
```

Adding the `ssd=true` label to additional nodes will case the `nginx-fast-storage` Pod to be deployed on those nodes. The inverse is also true: if a required label is removed from a node, the Pod will be removed by the DaemonSet controller.

 Removing labels from a node that are required by a DaemonSet's node selector will cause the Pod being managed by that DaemonSet to be removed from the node.

Updating a DaemonSet

DaemonSets are great for deploying services across an entire cluster, but what about upgrades? Prior to Kubernetes 1.6, the only way to update Pods managed by a DaemonSet was to update the DaemonSet and then manually delete each Pod that was managed by the DaemonSet so that it would be re-created with the new configuration. With the release of Kubernetes 1.6 DaemonSets gained an equivalent to the `Deployment` object that manages a DaemonSet rollout inside the cluster.

Updating a DaemonSet by Deleting Individual Pods

If you are running a pre-1.6 version of Kubernetes, you can perform a rolling delete of the Pods a `DaemonSet` manages using a `for` loop on your own machine to update one DaemonSet Pod every 60 seconds:

```
PODS=$(kubectl get pods -o jsonpath -template='{.items[*].metadata.name}'
for x in $PODS; do
  kubectl delete pods ${x}
  sleep 60
done
```

An alternative, easier approach is to just delete the entire DaemonSet and create a new DaemonSet with the updated configuration. However, this approach has a major drawback—downtime. When a DaemonSet is deleted all Pods managed by that DaemonSet will also be deleted. Depending on the size of your container images, recreating a DaemonSet may push you outside of your SLA thresholds, so it might be worth considering pulling updated container images across your cluster before updating a DaemonSet.

Rolling Update of a DaemonSet

With Kubernetes 1.6, DaemonSets can now be rolled out using the same rolling update strategy that deployments use. However, for reasons of backward compatability, the current default update strategy is the `delete` method described in the previous section. To set a DaemonSet to use the rolling update strategy, you need to configure the update strategy using the `spec.updateStrategy.type` field. That field should have the value `RollingUpdate`. When a DaemonSet has an update strategy of `RollingUpdate`, any change to the `spec.template` field (or subfields) in the DaemonSet will initiate a rolling update.

As with rolling updates of deployments (see Chapter 12), the rolling update strategy gradually updates members of a DaemonSet until all of the Pods are running the new configuration. There are two parameters that control the rolling update of a DaemonSet:

- `spec.minReadySeconds`, which determines how long a Pod must be "ready" before the rolling update proceeds to upgrade subsequent Pods
- `spec.updateStrategy.rollingUpdate.maxUnavailable`, which indicates how many Pods may be simultaneously updated by the rolling update

You will likely want to set `spec.minReadySeconds` to a reasonably long value, for example 30–60 seconds, to ensure that your Pod is truly healthy before the rollout proceeds.

The setting for `spec.updateStrategy.rollingUpdate.maxUnavailable` is more likely to be application-dependent. Setting it to `1` is a safe, general-purpose strategy, but it also takes a while to complete the rollout (number of nodes × `maxReadySec onds`). Increasing the maximum unavailability will make your rollout move faster, but increases the "blast radius" of a failed rollout. The characteristics of your application and cluster environment dictate the relative values of speed versus safety. A good approach might be to set `maxUnavailable` to 1 and only increase it if users or administrators complain about DaemonSet rollout speed.

Once a rolling update has started, you can use the `kubectl rollout` commands to see the current status of a DaemonSet rollout.

For example, `kubectl rollout status daemonSets my-daemon-set` will show the current rollout status of a DaemonSet named `my-daemon-set`.

Deleting a DaemonSet

Deleting a DaemonSet is pretty straightforward using the `kubectl delete` command. Just be sure to supply the correct name of the DaemonSet you would like to delete:

```
$ kubectl delete -f fluentd.yaml
```

 Deleting a DaemonSet will also delete all the Pods being managed by that DaemonSet. Set the `--cascade` flag to `false` to ensure only the DaemonSet is deleted and not the Pods.

Summary

DaemonSets provide an easy-to-use abstraction for running a set of Pods on every node in a Kubernetes cluster, or if the case requires it, on a subset of nodes based on labels. The DaemonSet provides its own controller and scheduler to ensure key services like monitoring agents are always up and running on the right nodes in your cluster.

For some applications, you simply want to schedule a certain number of replicas; you don't really care where they run as long as they have sufficient resources and distribution to operate reliably. However, there is a different class of applications, like agents and monitoring applications, that need to be present on every machine in a cluster to function properly. These DaemonSets aren't really traditional serving applications, but rather add additional capabilities and features to the Kubernetes cluster itself. Because the DaemonSet is an active declarative object managed by a controller, it makes it easy to declare your intent that an agent run on every machine without explicitly placing it on every machine. This is especially useful in the context of an autoscaled Kubernetes cluster where nodes may constantly be coming and going without user intervention. In such cases, the DaemonSet automatically adds the proper agents to each node as it is added to the cluster by the autoscaler.

## CHAPTER 10

Jobs

So far we have focused on long-running processes such as databases and web applications. These types of workloads run until either they are upgraded or the service is no longer needed. While long-running processes make up the large majority of workloads that run on a Kubernetes cluster, there is often a need to run short lived, one-off tasks. The Job object is made for handling these types of tasks.

A Job creates Pods that run until successful termination (i.e., exit with 0). In contrast, a regular Pod will continually restart regardless of its exit code. Jobs are useful for things you only want to do once, such as database migrations or batch jobs. If run as a regular Pod, your database migration task would run in a loop, continually repopulating the database after every exit.

In this chapter we explore the most common Job patterns afforded by Kubernetes. We will also leverage these patterns in real-life scenarios.

The Job Object

The Job object is responsible for creating and managing pods defined in a template in the Job specification. These pods generally run until successful completion. The Job object coordinates running a number of pods in parallel.

If the Pod fails before a successful termination, the Job controller will create a new Pod based on the Pod template in the Job specification. Given that Pods have to be scheduled, there is a chance that your Job will not execute if the required resources are not found by the scheduler. Also, due to the nature of distributed systems there is a small chance, during certain failure scenarios, that duplicate pods will be created for a specific task.

Job Patterns

Jobs are designed to manage batch-like workloads where work items are processed by one or more Pods. By default each Job runs a single Pod once until successful termination. This Job pattern is defined by two primary attributes of a Job, namely the number of Job completions and the number of Pods to run in parallel. In the case of the "run once until completion" pattern, the `completions` and `parallelism` parameters are set to 1.

Table 10-1 highlights Job patterns based on the combination of `completions` and `parallelism` for a Job configuration.

Table 10-1. Job patterns

Type	Use case	Behavior	completions	parallelism
One shot	Database migrations	A single pod running once until successful termination	1	1
Parallel fixed completions	Multiple pods processing a set of work in parallel	One or more Pods running one or more times until reaching a fixed completion count	1+	1+
Work queue: parallel Jobs	Multiple pods processing from a centralized work queue	One or more Pods running once until successful termination	1	2+

One Shot

One-shot Jobs provide a way to run a single Pod once until successful termination. While this may sound like an easy task, there is some work involved in pulling this off. First, a Pod must be created and submitted to the Kubernetes API. This is done using a Pod template defined in the Job configuration. Once a Job is up and running, the Pod backing the Job must be monitored for successful termination. A Job can fail for any number of reasons including an application error, an uncaught exception during runtime, or a node failure before the Job has a chance to complete. In all cases the Job controller is responsible for recreating the Pod until a successful termination occurs.

There are multiple ways to create a one-shot Job in Kubernetes. The easiest is to use the `kubectl` command-line tool:

```
$ kubectl run -i oneshot \
  --image=gcr.io/kuar-demo/kuard-amd64:1 \
  --restart=OnFailure \
  -- --keygen-enable \
     --keygen-exit-on-complete \
     --keygen-num-to-gen 10

...
```

```
(ID 0) Workload starting
(ID 0 1/10) Item done: SHA256:nAsUsG54XoKRkJwyN+OShkUPKew3mwq7OCc
(ID 0 2/10) Item done: SHA256:HVKX1ANns6SgF/er1lyo+ZCdnB8geFGt0/8
(ID 0 3/10) Item done: SHA256:irjCLRov3mTT0P0JfsvUyhKRQ1TdGR8H1jg
(ID 0 4/10) Item done: SHA256:nbQAIVY/yrhmEGk3Ui2sAHuxb/o6mYO0qRk
(ID 0 5/10) Item done: SHA256:CCpBoXNlXOMQvR2v38yqimXGAa/w2Tym+aI
(ID 0 6/10) Item done: SHA256:wEY2TTIDz4ATjcr1iimxavCzZzNjRmbOQp8
(ID 0 7/10) Item done: SHA256:t3JSrCt7sQweBgqG5CrbMoBulwk4lfDWiTI
(ID 0 8/10) Item done: SHA256:E84/Vze7KKyjCh9OZh02MkXJGoty9PhaCec
(ID 0 9/10) Item done: SHA256:UOmYex79qqbI1MhcIfG4hDnGKonlsij2k3s
(ID 0 10/10) Item done: SHA256:WCR8wIGOFag84Bsa8f/9QHuKqF+0mEnCADY
(ID 0) Workload exiting
```

There are some things to note here:

- The `-i` option to kubectl indicates that this is an interactive command. kubectl will wait until the Job is running and then show the log output from the first (and in this case only) pod in the Job.

- `--restart=OnFailure` is the option that tells kubectl to create a Job object.

- All of the options after `--` are command-line arguments to the container image. These instruct our test server (kuard) to generate 10 4,096-bit SSH keys and then exit.

- Your output may not match this exactly. kubectl often misses the first couple of lines of output with the `-i` option.

After the Job has completed, the Job object and related Pod are still around. This is so that you can inspect the log output. Note that this Job won't show up in kubectl `get jobs` unless you pass the `-a` flag. Without this flag kubectl hides completed Jobs. Delete the Job before continuing:

```
$ kubectl delete jobs oneshot
```

The other option for creating a one-shot Job is using a configuration file, as shown in Example 10-1.

Example 10-1. job-oneshot.yaml

```
apiVersion: batch/v1
kind: Job
metadata:
  name: oneshot
  labels:
    chapter: jobs
spec:
  template:
    metadata:
      labels:
        chapter: jobs
```

```
spec:
  containers:
  - name: kuard
    image: gcr.io/kuar-demo/kuard-amd64:1
    imagePullPolicy: Always
    args:
    - "--keygen-enable"
    - "--keygen-exit-on-complete"
    - "--keygen-num-to-gen=10"
  restartPolicy: OnFailure
```

Submit the job using the kubectl apply command:

```
$ kubectl apply -f job-oneshot.yaml
job "oneshot" created
```

Then describe the oneshot job:

```
$ kubectl describe jobs oneshot

Name:            oneshot
Namespace:       default
Image(s):        gcr.io/kuar-demo/kuard-amd64:1
Selector:        controller-uid=cf87484b-e664-11e6-8222-42010a8a007b
Parallelism:     1
Completions:     1
Start Time:      Sun, 29 Jan 2017 12:52:13 -0800
Labels:          Job=oneshot
Pods Statuses:   0 Running / 1 Succeeded / 0 Failed
No volumes.
Events:
   ... Reason           Message
   ... ------           -------
   ... SuccessfulCreate Created pod: oneshot-4kfdt
```

You can view the results of the Job by looking at the logs of the pod that was created:

```
$ kubectl logs oneshot-4kfdt

...
Serving on :8080
(ID 0) Workload starting
(ID 0 1/10) Item done: SHA256:+r6b4W81DbEjxMcD3LHjU+EIGnLEzbpxITKn8IqhkPI
(ID 0 2/10) Item done: SHA256:mzHewajaY1KA8VluSLOnNMk9fDE5zdn7vvBS5Ne8AxM
(ID 0 3/10) Item done: SHA256:TRtEQHfflJmwkqnNyGgQm/IvXNykSBIg8c03h0g3onE
(ID 0 4/10) Item done: SHA256:tSwPYH/J347il/mgqTxRRdeZcOazEtgZlA8A3/HWbro
(ID 0 5/10) Item done: SHA256:IP8XtguJ6GbWwLHqjKecVfdS96B17nnO21I/TNc1j9k
(ID 0 6/10) Item done: SHA256:ZfNxdQvuST/6ZzEVkyxdRG98p73c/5TM99SEbPeRWfc
(ID 0 7/10) Item done: SHA256:tH+CNl/IUl/HUuKdMsq2XEmDQ8oAvmhMO6Iwj8ZEOj0
(ID 0 8/10) Item done: SHA256:3GfsUaALVEHQcGNLBOu4Qd1zqqqJ8j738i5r+I5XwVI
(ID 0 9/10) Item done: SHA256:5wV4L/xEiHSJXwLUT2fHf0SCKM2g3XH3sVtNbgskCXw
(ID 0 10/10) Item done: SHA256:bPqqOonwSbjzLqe9ZuVRmZkz+DBjaNTZ9HwmQhbdWLI
(ID 0) Workload exiting
```

Congratulations, your job has run successfully!

 You may have noticed that we didn't specify any labels when creating the Job object. Like with other controllers (DaemonSet, Replica-Sets, deployments, etc.) that use labels to identify a set of Pods, unexpected behaviors can happen if a pod is reused across objects.

Because Jobs have a finite beginning and ending, it is common for users to create many of them. This makes picking unique labels more difficult and more critical. For this reason, the Job object will automatically pick a unique label and use it to identify the pods it creates. In advanced scenarios (such as swapping out a running Job without killing the pods it is managing) users can choose to turn off this automatic behavior and manually specify labels and selectors.

Pod failure

We just saw how a Job can complete successfully. But what happens if something fails? Let's try that out and see what happens.

Let's modify the arguments to kuard in our configuration file to cause it to fail out with a nonzero exit code after generating three keys, as shown in Example 10-2.

Example 10-2. job-oneshot-failure1.yaml

```
...
spec:
  template:
    spec:
      containers:
        ...
        args:
        - "--keygen-enable"
        - "--keygen-exit-on-complete"
        - "--keygen-exit-code=1"
        - "--keygen-num-to-gen=3"
...
```

Now launch this with kubectl apply -f jobs-oneshot-failure1.yaml. Let it run for a bit and then look at the pod status:

```
$ kubectl get pod -a -l job-name=oneshot

NAME            READY   STATUS             RESTARTS   AGE
oneshot-3ddk0   0/1     CrashLoopBackOff   4          3m
```

Here we see that the same Pod has restarted four times. Kubernetes is in CrashLoop BackOff for this Pod. It is not uncommon to have a bug someplace that causes a program to crash as soon as it starts. In that case, Kubernetes will wait a bit before restarting the pod to avoid a crash loop eating resources on the node. This is all handled local to the node by the kubelet without the Job being involved at all.

Kill the Job (kubectl delete jobs oneshot), and let's try something else. Modify the config file again and change the restartPolicy from OnFailure to Never. Launch this with kubectl apply -f jobs-oneshot-failure2.yaml.

If we let this run for a bit and then look at related pods we'll find something interesting:

```
$ kubectl get pod -l job-name=oneshot -a

NAME            READY     STATUS    RESTARTS   AGE oneshot-0wm49   0/1
Error    0           1m oneshot-6h9s2   0/1    Error    0           39s
oneshot-hkzw0   1/1       Running   0          6s oneshot-k5swz  0/1
Error    0           28s oneshot-m1rdw   0/1    Error    0           19s
oneshot-x157b   0/1       Error     0          57s
```

What we see is that we have multiple pods here that have errored out. By setting restartPolicy: Never we are telling the kubelet not to restart the Pod on failure, but rather just declare the Pod as failed. The Job object then notices and creates a replacement Pod. If you aren't careful, this'll create a lot of "junk" in your cluster. For this reason, we suggest you use restartPolicy: OnFailure so failed Pods are rerun in place.

Clean this up with kubectl delete jobs oneshot.

So far we've seen a program fail by exiting with a nonzero exit code. But workers can fail in other ways. Specifically, they can get stuck and not make any forward progress. To help cover this case, you can use liveness probes with Jobs. If the liveness probe policy determines that a Pod is dead, it'll be restarted/replaced for you.

Parallelism

Generating keys can be slow. Let's start a bunch of workers together to make key generation faster. We're going to use a combination of the completions and parallelism parameters. Our goal is to generate 100 keys by having 10 runs of kuard with each run generating 10 keys. But we don't want to swamp our cluster, so we'll limit ourselves to only five pods at a time.

This translates to setting completions to 10 and parallelism to 5. The config is shown in Example 10-2.

Example 10-3. job-parallel.yaml

```yaml
apiVersion: batch/v1
kind: Job
metadata:
  name: parallel
  labels:
    chapter: jobs
spec:
  parallelism: 5
  completions: 10
  template:
    metadata:
      labels:
        chapter: jobs
    spec:
      containers:
      - name: kuard
        image: gcr.io/kuar-demo/kuard-amd64:1
        imagePullPolicy: Always
        args:
        - "--keygen-enable"
        - "--keygen-exit-on-complete"
        - "--keygen-num-to-gen=10"
      restartPolicy: OnFailure
```

Start it up:

```
$ kubectl apply -f job-parallel.yaml
job "parallel" created
```

Now watch as the pods come up, do their thing, and exit. New pods are created until 10 have completed altogether. Here we use the --watch flag to have kubectl stay around and list changes as they happen:

```
$ kubectl get pods -w
NAME              READY    STATUS            RESTARTS   AGE
parallel-55tlv    1/1      Running           0          5s
parallel-5s7s9    1/1      Running           0          5s
parallel-jp7bj    1/1      Running           0          5s
parallel-lssmn    1/1      Running           0          5s
parallel-qxcxp    1/1      Running           0          5s
NAME              READY    STATUS            RESTARTS   AGE
parallel-jp7bj    0/1      Completed         0          26s
parallel-tzp9n    0/1      Pending           0          0s
parallel-tzp9n    0/1      Pending           0          0s
parallel-tzp9n    0/1      ContainerCreating 0          1s
parallel-tzp9n    1/1      Running           0          1s
parallel-tzp9n    0/1      Completed         0          48s
parallel-x1kmr    0/1      Pending           0          0s
parallel-x1kmr    0/1      Pending           0          0s
parallel-x1kmr    0/1      ContainerCreating 0          0s
```

```
parallel-x1kmr    1/1    Running            0         1s
parallel-5s7s9    0/1    Completed      0          1m
parallel-tprfj    0/1    Pending            0         0s
parallel-tprfj    0/1    Pending            0         0s
parallel-tprfj    0/1    ContainerCreating  0              0s
parallel-tprfj    1/1    Running            0         2s
parallel-x1kmr    0/1    Completed      0          52s
parallel-bgvz5    0/1    Pending            0         0s
parallel-bgvz5    0/1    Pending            0         0s
parallel-bgvz5    0/1    ContainerCreating  0              0s
parallel-bgvz5    1/1    Running            0         2s
parallel-qxcxp    0/1    Completed      0          2m
parallel-xplw2    0/1    Pending            0         1s
parallel-xplw2    0/1    Pending            0         1s
parallel-xplw2    0/1    ContainerCreating  0              1s
parallel-xplw2    1/1    Running            0         3s
parallel-bgvz5    0/1    Completed      0          40s
parallel-55tlv    0/1    Completed      0          2m
parallel-lssmn    0/1    Completed      0          2m
```

Feel free to poke around at the completed Jobs and check out their logs to see the fingerprints of the keys they generated. Clean up by deleting the finished Job object with kubectl delete job parallel.

Work Queues

A common use case for Jobs is to process work from a work queue. In this scenario, some task creates a number of work items and publishes them to a work queue. A worker Job can be run to process each work item until the work queue is empty (Figure 10-1).

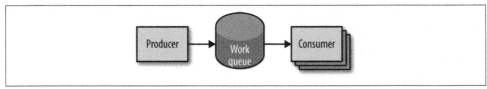

Figure 10-1. Parallel jobs

Starting a work queue

We start by launching a centralized work queue service. kuard has a simple memory-based work queue system built in. We will start an instance of kuard to act as a coordinator for all the work to be done.

Create a simple ReplicaSet to manage a singleton work queue daemon. We are using a ReplicaSet to ensure that a new Pod will get created in the face of machine failure, as shown in Example 10-4.

Example 10-4. rs-queue.yaml

```
apiVersion: extensions/v1beta1
kind: ReplicaSet
metadata:
  labels:
    app: work-queue
    component: queue
    chapter: jobs
  name: queue
spec:
  replicas: 1
  template:
    metadata:
      labels:
        app: work-queue
        component: queue
        chapter: jobs
    spec:
      containers:
      - name: queue
        image: "gcr.io/kuar-demo/kuard-amd64:1"
        imagePullPolicy: Always
```

Run the work queue with the following command:

```
$ kubectl apply -f rs-queue.yaml
```

At this point the work queue daemon should be up and running. Let's use port forwarding to connect to it. Leave this command running in a terminal window:

```
$ QUEUE_POD=$(kubectl get pods -l app=work-queue,component=queue \
    -o jsonpath='{.items[0].metadata.name}')
$ kubectl port-forward $QUEUE_POD 8080:8080
Forwarding from 127.0.0.1:8080 -> 8080
Forwarding from [::1]:8080 -> 8080
```

You can open your browser to *http://localhost:8080* and see the kuard interface. Switch to the "MemQ Server" tab to keep an eye on what is going on.

With the work queue server in place, we should expose it using a service. This will make it easy for producers and consumers to locate the work queue via DNS, as Example 10-5 shows.

Example 10-5. service-queue.yaml

```
apiVersion: v1
kind: Service
metadata:
  labels:
    app: work-queue
    component: queue
```

```
      chapter: jobs
    name: queue
  spec:
    ports:
    - port: 8080
      protocol: TCP
      targetPort: 8080
    selector:
      app: work-queue
      component: queue
```

Create the queue service with kubectl:

```
$ kubectl apply -f service-queue.yaml
service "queue" created
```

Loading up the queue

We are now ready to put a bunch of work items in the queue. For the sake of simplicity we'll just use curl to drive the API for the work queue server and insert a bunch of work items. curl will communicate to the work queue through the kubectl port-forward we set up earlier, as shown in Example 10-6.

Example 10-6. load-queue.sh

```
# Create a work queue called 'keygen'
curl -X PUT localhost:8080/memq/server/queues/keygen

# Create 100 work items and load up the queue.
for i in work-item-{0..99}; do
  curl -X POST localhost:8080/memq/server/queues/keygen/enqueue \
    -d "$i"
done
```

Run these commands, and you should see 100 JSON objects output to your terminal with a unique message identifier for each work item. You can confirm the status of the queue by looking at the "MemQ Server" tab in the UI, or you can ask the work queue API directly:

```
$ curl 127.0.0.1:8080/memq/server/stats
{
    "kind": "stats",
    "queues": [
        {
            "depth": 100,
            "dequeued": 0,
            "drained": 0,
            "enqueued": 100,
            "name": "keygen"
        }
```

```
      ]
  }
```

Now we are ready to kick off a Job to consume the work queue until it's empty.

Creating the consumer job

This is where things get interesting! kuard is also able to act in consumer mode. Here we set it up to draw work items from the work queue, create a key, and then exit once the queue is empty, as shown in Example 10-7.

Example 10-7. job-consumers.yaml

```
apiVersion: batch/v1
kind: Job
metadata:
  labels:
    app: message-queue
    component: consumer
    chapter: jobs
  name: consumers
spec:
  parallelism: 5
  template:
    metadata:
      labels:
        app: message-queue
        component: consumer
        chapter: jobs
    spec:
      containers:
      - name: worker
        image: "gcr.io/kuar-demo/kuard-amd64:1"
        imagePullPolicy: Always
        args:
        - "--keygen-enable"
        - "--keygen-exit-on-complete"
        - "--keygen-memq-server=http://queue:8080/memq/server"
        - "--keygen-memq-queue=keygen"
      restartPolicy: OnFailure
```

We are telling the Job to start up five pods in parallel. As the completions parameter is unset, we put the Job into a worker pool mode. Once the first pod exits with a zero exit code, the Job will start winding down and will not start any new Pods. This means that none of the workers should exit until the work is done and they are all in the process of finishing up.

Create the consumers Job:

```
$ kubectl apply -f job-consumers.yaml
job "consumers" created
```

Once the Job has been created you can view the pods backing the Job:

```
$ kubectl get pods
NAME              READY   STATUS    RESTARTS   AGE
queue-43s87       1/1     Running   0          5m
consumers-6wjxc   1/1     Running   0          2m
consumers-7l5mh   1/1     Running   0          2m
consumers-hvz42   1/1     Running   0          2m
consumers-pc8hr   1/1     Running   0          2m
consumers-w20cc   1/1     Running   0          2m
```

Note there are five pods running in parallel. These pods will continue to run until the work queue is empty. You can watch as it happens in the UI on the work queue server. As the queue empties, the consumer pods will exit cleanly and the `consumers` Job will be considered complete.

Cleaning up

Using labels we can clean up all of the stuff we created in this section:

```
$ kubectl delete rs,svc,job -l chapter=jobs
```

Summary

On a single cluster, Kubernetes can handle both long-running workloads such as web applications and short-lived workloads such as batch jobs. The Job abstraction allows you to model batch job patterns ranging from simple one-time tasks to parallel jobs that process many items until work has been exhausted.

Jobs are a low-level primitive and can be used directly for simple workloads. However, Kubernetes is built from the ground up to be extensible by higher-level objects. Jobs are no exception; they can easily be used by higher-level orchestration systems to take on more complex tasks.

## CHAPTER 11

ConfigMaps and Secrets

It is a good practice to make container images as reusable as possible. The same image should be able to be used for development, staging, and production. It is even better if the same image is general purpose enough to be used across applications and services. Testing and versioning get riskier and more complicated if images need to be recreated for each new environment. But then how do we specialize the use of that image at runtime?

This is where ConfigMaps and secrets come into play. ConfigMaps are used to provide configuration information for workloads. This can either be fine-grained information (a short string) or a composite value in the form of a file. Secrets are similar to ConfigMaps but focused on making sensitive information available to the workload. They can be used for things like credentials or TLS certificates.

ConfigMaps

One way to think of a ConfigMap is as a Kubernetes object that defines a small filesystem. Another way is as a set of variables that can be used when defining the environment or command line for your containers. The key thing is that the ConfigMap is combined with the Pod right before it is run. This means that the container image and the pod definition itself can be reused across many apps by just changing the ConfigMap that is used.

Creating ConfigMaps

Let's jump right in and create a ConfigMap. Like many objects in Kubernetes, you can create these in an immediate, imperative way or you can create them from a manifest on disk. We'll start with the imperative method.

First, suppose we have a file on disk (called *my-config.txt*) that we want to make available to the Pod in question, as shown in Example 11-1.

Example 11-1. my-config.txt

```
# This is a sample config file that I might use to configure an application
parameter1 = value1
parameter2 = value2
```

Next, let's create a ConfigMap with that file. We'll also add a couple of simple key/value pairs here. These are referred to as literal values on the command line:

```
$ kubectl create configmap my-config \
  --from-file=my-config.txt \
  --from-literal=extra-param=extra-value \
  --from-literal=another-param=another-value
```

The equivalent YAML for the ConfigMap object we just created is:

```
$ kubectl get configmaps my-config -o yaml

apiVersion: v1
data:
  another-param: another-value
  extra-param: extra-value
  my-config.txt: |
    # This is a sample config file that I might use to configure an application
    parameter1 = value1
    parameter2 = value2
kind: ConfigMap
metadata:
  creationTimestamp: ...
  name: my-config
  namespace: default
  resourceVersion: "13556"
  selfLink: /api/v1/namespaces/default/configmaps/my-config
  uid: 3641c553-f7de-11e6-98c9-06135271a273
```

As you can see, the ConfigMap is really just some key/value pairs stored in an object. The interesting stuff happens when you try to *use* a ConfigMap.

Using a ConfigMap

There are three main ways to use a ConfigMap:

Filesystem
> You can mount a ConfigMap into a Pod. A file is created for each entry based on the key name. The contents of that file are set to the value.

Environment variable

A ConfigMap can be used to dynamically set the value of an environment variable.

Command-line argument

Kubernetes supports dynamically creating the command line for a container based on ConfigMap values.

Let's create a manifest for `kuard` that pulls all of these together, as shown in Example 11-2.

Example 11-2. kuard-config.yaml

```yaml
apiVersion: v1
kind: Pod
metadata:
  name: kuard-config
spec:
  containers:
    - name: test-container
      image: gcr.io/kuar-demo/kuard-amd64:1
      imagePullPolicy: Always
      command:
        - "/kuard"
        - "$(EXTRA_PARAM)"
      env:
        - name: ANOTHER_PARAM
          valueFrom:
            configMapKeyRef:
              name: my-config
              key: another-param
        - name: EXTRA_PARAM
          valueFrom:
            configMapKeyRef:
              name: my-config
              key: extra-param
      volumeMounts:
        - name: config-volume
          mountPath: /config
  volumes:
    - name: config-volume
      configMap:
        name: my-config
  restartPolicy: Never
```

For the filesystem method, we create a new volume inside the pod and give it the name `config-volume`. We then define this volume to be a ConfigMap volume and point at the ConfigMap to mount. We have to specify where this gets mounted into the `kuard` container with a `volumeMount`. In this case we are mounting it at `/config`.

Environment variables are specified with a special `valueFrom` member. This references the ConfigMap and the data key to use within that ConfigMap.

Command-line arguments build on environment variables. Kubernetes will perform the correct substitution with a special `$(<env-var-name>)` syntax.

Run this Pod and let's port-forward to examine how the app sees the world:

```
$ kubectl apply -f kuard-config.yaml
$ kubectl port-forward kuard-config 8080
```

Now point your browser at *http://localhost:8080*. We can look at how we've injected configuration values into the program in all three ways.

Click on the "Server Env" tab on the left. This will show the command line that the app was launched with along with its environment, as shown in Figure 11-1.

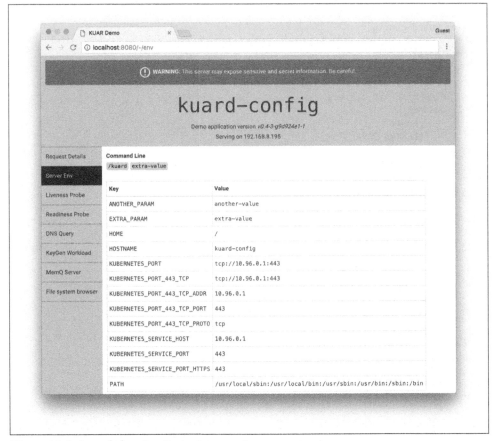

Figure 11-1. kuard showing its environment

Here we can see that we've added two environment variables (ANOTHER_PARAM and EXTRA_PARAM) whose values are set via the ConfigMap. Furthermore, we've added an argument to the command line of kuard based on the EXTRA_PARAM value.

Next, click on the "File system browser" tab (Figure 11-2). This lets you explore the filesystem as the application sees it. You should see an entry called /config. This is a volume created based on our ConfigMap. If you navigate into that, you'll see that a file has been created for each entry of the ConfigMap. You'll also see some hidden files (prepended with ..) that are used to do a clean swap of new values when the ConfigMap is updated.

Figure 11-2. The /config directory as seen through kuard

Secrets

While ConfigMaps are great for most configuration data, there is certain data that is extra-sensitive. This can include passwords, security tokens, or other types of private keys. Collectively, we call this type of data "secrets." Kubernetes has native support for storing and handling this data with care.

Secrets enable container images to be created without bundling sensitive data. This allows containers to remain portable across environments. Secrets are exposed to pods via explicit declaration in pod manifests and the Kubernetes API. In this way the Kubernetes secrets API provides an application-centric mechanism for exposing sensitive configuration information to applications in a way that's easy to audit and leverages native OS isolation primitives.

 Depending on your requirements, Kubernetes secrets may not be secure enough for you. As of Kubernetes version 1.6, anyone with root access on any node has access to all secrets in the cluster. While Kubernetes utilizes native OS containerization primitives to only expose Pods to secrets they are supposed to see, isolation between nodes is still a work in progress.

Kubernetes version 1.7 improves this situation quite a bit. When properly configured, it both encrypts stored secrets and restricts the secrets that each individual node has access to.

The remainder of this section will explore how to create and manage Kubernetes secrets, and also lay out best practices for exposing secrets to pods that require them.

Creating Secrets

Secrets are created using the Kubernetes API or the `kubectl` command-line tool. Secrets hold one or more data elements as a collection of key/value pairs.

In this section we will create a secret to store a TLS key and certificate for the `kuard` application that meets the storage requirements listed above.

 The kuard container image does not bundle a TLS certificate or key. This allows the `kuard` container to remain portable across environments and distributable through public Docker repositories.

The first step in creating a secret is to obtain the raw data we want to store. The TLS key and certificate for the kuard application can be downloaded by running the following commands (please don't use these certificates outside of this example):

```
$ curl -O https://storage.googleapis.com/kuar-demo/kuard.crt
$ curl -O https://storage.googleapis.com/kuar-demo/kuard.key
```

With the *kuard.crt* and *kuard.key* files stored locally, we are ready to create a secret. Create a secret named `kuard-tls` using the `create secret` command:

```
$ kubectl create secret generic kuard-tls \
  --from-file=kuard.crt \
  --from-file=kuard.key
```

The kuard-tls secret has been created with two data elements. Run the following command to get details:

```
$ kubectl describe secrets kuard-tls

Name:         kuard-tls
Namespace:    default
Labels:       <none>
Annotations:  <none>

Type:         Opaque

Data
====
kuard.crt:    1050 bytes
kuard.key:    1679 bytes
```

With the kuard-tls secret in place, we can consume it from a pod by using a secrets volume.

Consuming Secrets

Secrets can be consumed using the Kubernetes REST API by applications that know how to call that API directly. However, our goal is to keep applications portable. Not only should they run well in Kubernetes, but they should run, unmodified, on other platforms.

Instead of accessing secrets through the API server, we can use a *secrets volume*.

Secrets volumes

Secret data can be exposed to pods using the secrets volume type. Secrets volumes are managed by the kubelet and are created at pod creation time. Secrets are stored on tmpfs volumes (aka RAM disks) and, as such, are not written to disk on nodes.

Each data element of a secret is stored in a separate file under the target mount point specified in the volume mount. The kuard-tls secret contains two data elements: *kuard.crt* and *kuard.key*. Mounting the kuard-tls secrets volume to /tls results in the following files:

```
/tls/cert.pem
/tls/key.pem
```

The following pod manifest (Example 11-3) demonstrates how to declare a secrets volume, which exposes the kuard-tls secret to the kuard container under /tls.

Example 11-3. kuard-secret.yaml

```
apiVersion: v1
kind: Pod
metadata:
  name: kuard-tls
spec:
  containers:
    - name: kuard-tls
      image: gcr.io/kuar-demo/kuard-amd64:1
      imagePullPolicy: Always
      volumeMounts:
      - name: tls-certs
        mountPath: "/tls"
        readOnly: true
  volumes:
    - name: tls-certs
      secret:
        secretName: kuard-tls
```

Create the kuard-tls pod using kubectl and observe the log output from the running pod:

```
$ kubectl apply -f kuard-secret.yaml
```

Connect to the pod by running:

```
$ kubectl port-forward kuard-tls 8443:8443
```

Now navigate your browser to *https://localhost:8443*. You should see some invalid certificate warnings as this is a self-signed certificate for *kuard.example.com*. If you navigate past this warning, you should see the kuard server hosted via HTTPS. Use the "File system browser" tab to find the certificates on disk.

Private Docker Registries

A special use case for secrets is to store access credentials for private Docker registries. Kubernetes supports using images stored on private registries, but access to those images requires credentials. Private images can be stored across one or more private registries. This presents a challenge for managing credentials for each private registry on every possible node in the cluster.

Image pull secrets leverage the secrets API to automate the distribution of private registry credentials. Image pull secrets are stored just like normal secrets but are consumed through the spec.imagePullSecrets Pod specification field.

Use the create secret docker-registry to create this special kind of secret:

```
$ kubectl create secret docker-registry my-image-pull-secret \
  --docker-username=<username> \
```

```
    --docker-password=<password> \
    --docker-email=<email-address>
```

Enable access to the private repository by referencing the image pull secret in the pod manifest file, as shown in Example 11-4.

Example 11-4. kuard-secret-ips.yaml

```
apiVersion: v1
kind: Pod
metadata:
  name: kuard-tls
spec:
  containers:
    - name: kuard-tls
      image: gcr.io/kuar-demo/kuard-amd64:1
      imagePullPolicy: Always
      volumeMounts:
      - name: tls-certs
        mountPath: "/tls"
        readOnly: true
  imagePullSecrets:
  - name:  my-image-pull-secret
  volumes:
    - name: tls-certs
      secret:
        secretName: kuard-tls
```

Naming Constraints

The key names for data items inside of a secret or ConfigMap are defined to map to valid environment variable names. They may begin with a dot followed by a letter or number. Following characters include dots, dashes, and underscores. Dots cannot be repeated and dots and underscores or dashes cannot be adjacent to each other. More formally, this means that they must conform to the regular expression `[.]?[a-zA-Z0-9]([.]?[-_a-zA-Z0-9]*[a-zA-Z0-9])*`. Some examples of valid and invalid names for ConfigMaps or secrets are given in Table 11-1.

Table 11-1. ConfigMap and secret key examples

Valid key name	Invalid key name
`.auth_token`	`Token..properties`
`Key.pem`	`auth file.json`
`config_file`	`_password.txt`

When selecting a key name consider that these keys can be exposed to pods via a volume mount. Pick a name that is going to make sense when specified on a command line or in a config file. Storing a TLS key as key.pem is more clear than tls-key when configuring applications to access secrets.

ConfigMap data values are simple UTF-8 text specified directly in the manifest. As of Kubernetes 1.6, ConfigMaps are unable to store binary data.

Secret data values hold arbitrary data encoded using base64. The use of base64 encoding makes it possible to store binary data. This does, however, make it more difficult to manage secrets that are stored in YAML files as the base64-encoded value must be put in the YAML.

Managing ConfigMaps and Secrets

Secrets and ConfigMaps are managed through the Kubernetes API. The usual `create`, `delete`, `get`, and `describe` commands work for manipulating these objects.

Listing

You can use the `kubectl get secrets` command to list all secrets in the current namespace:

```
$ kubectl get secrets

NAME                 TYPE                                  DATA   AGE
default-token-f5jq2  kubernetes.io/service-account-token   3      1h
kuard-tls            Opaque                                2      20m
```

Similarly, you can list all of the ConfigMaps in a namespace:

```
$ kubectl get configmaps

NAME       DATA   AGE
my-config  3      1m
```

`kubectl describe` can be used to get more details on a single object:

```
$ kubectl describe configmap my-config

Name:         my-config
Namespace:    default
Labels:       <none>
Annotations:  <none>

Data
====
another-param:  13 bytes
```

```
extra-param:    11 bytes
my-config.txt:  116 bytes
```

Finally, you can see the raw data (including values in secrets!) with something like `kubectl get configmap my-config -o yaml` or `kubectl get secret kuard-tls -o yaml`.

Creating

The easiest way to create a secret or a ConfigMap is via `kubectl create secret generic` or `kubectl create configmap`. There are a variety of ways to specify the data items that go into the secret or ConfigMap. These can be combined in a single command:

`--from-file=<filename>`
Load from the file with the secret data key the same as the filename.

`--from-file=<key>=<filename>`
Load from the file with the secret data key explicitly specified.

`--from-file=<directory>`
Load all the files in the specified directory where the filename is an acceptable key name.

`--from-literal=<key>=<value>`
Use the specified key/value pair directly.

Updating

You can update a ConfigMap or secret and have it reflected in running programs. There is no need to restart if the application is configured to reread configuration values. This is a rare feature but might be something you put in your own applications.

The following are three ways to update ConfigMaps or secrets.

Update from file

If you have a manifest for your ConfigMap or secret, you can just edit it directly and push a new version with `kubectl replace -f <filename>`. You can also use `kubectl apply -f <filename>` if you previously created the resource with `kubectl apply`.

Due to the way that datafiles are encoded into these objects, updating a configuration can be a bit cumbersome as there is no provision in `kubectl` to load data from an external file. The data must be stored directly in the YAML manifest.

The most common use case is when the ConfigMap is defined as part of a directory or list of resources and everything is created and updated together. Oftentimes these manifests will be checked into source control.

 It is generally a bad idea to check secret YAML files into source control. It is too easy to push these files someplace public and leak your secrets.

Recreate and update

If you store the inputs into your ConfigMaps or secrets as separate files on disk (as opposed to embedded into YAML directly), you can use kubectl to recreate the manifest and then use it to update the object.

This will look something like this:

```
$ kubectl create secret generic kuard-tls \
  --from-file=kuard.crt --from-file=kuard.key \
  --dry-run -o yaml | kubectl replace -f -
```

This command line first creates a new secret with the same name as our existing secret. If we just stopped there, the Kubernetes API server would return an error complaining that we are trying to create a secret that already exists. Instead, we tell kubectl not to actually send the data to the server but instead to dump the YAML that it *would have* sent to the API server to stdout. We then pipe that to kubectl replace and use -f - to tell it to read from stdin. In this way we can update a secret from files on disk without having to manually base64-encode data.

Edit current version

The final way to update a ConfigMap is to use kubectl edit to bring up a version of the ConfigMap in your editor so you can tweak it (you could also do this with a secret, but you'd be stuck managing the base64 encoding of values on your own):

```
$ kubectl edit configmap my-config
```

You should see the ConfigMap definition in your editor. Make your desired changes and then save and close your editor. The new version of the object will be pushed to the Kubernetes API server.

Live updates

Once a ConfigMap or secret is updated using the API, it'll be automatically pushed to all volumes that use that ConfigMap or secret. It may take a few seconds, but the file listing and contents of the files, as seen by kuard, will be updated with these new values. Using this live update feature you can update the configuration of applications without restarting them.

Currently there is no built-in way to signal an application when a new version of a ConfigMap is deployed. It is up to the application (or some helper script) to look for the config files to change and reload them.

Using the file browser in kuard (accessed through kubectl port-forward) is a great way to interactively play with dynamically updating secrets and ConfigMaps.

Summary

ConfigMaps and secrets are a great way to provide dynamic configuration in your application. They allow you to create a container image (and pod definition) once and reuse it in different contexts. This can include using the exact same image as you move from dev to staging to production. It can also include using a single image across multiple teams and services. Separating configuration from application code will make your applications more reliable and reusable.

## CHAPTER 12

Deployments

So far, you have seen how to package your application as a container, create a replicated set of these containers, and use services to load-balance traffic to your service. All of these objects are used to build a single instance of your application. They do little to help you manage the daily or weekly cadence of releasing new versions of your application. Indeed, both Pods and ReplicaSets are expected to be tied to specific container images that don't change.

The Deployment object exists to manage the release of new versions. Deployments represent deployed applications in a way that transcends any particular software version of the application. Additionally, Deployments enable you to easily move from one version of your code to the next version of your code. This "rollout" process is configurable and careful. It waits for a user-configurable amount of time between upgrading individual Pods. It also uses health checks to ensure that the new version of the application is operating correctly, and stops the deployment if too many failures occur.

Using Deployments you can simply and reliably roll out new software versions without downtime or errors. The actual mechanics of the software rollout performed by a Deployment is controlled by a Deployment controller that runs in the Kubernetes cluster itself. This means you can let a Deployment proceed unattended and it will still operate correctly and safely. This makes it easy to integrate Deployments with numerous continuous delivery tools and services. Further, running server-side makes it safe to perform a rollout from places with poor or intermittent internet connectivity. Imagine rolling out a new version of your software from your phone while riding on the subway. Deployments make this possible and safe!

When Kubernetes was first released, one of the most popular demonstrations of its power was the "rolling update," which showed how you could use a single command to seamlessly update a running application without taking any downtime or losing requests. This original demo was based on the `kubectl rolling-update` command, which is still available in the command-line tool, but its functionality has largely been subsumed by the `Deployment` object.

Your First Deployment

At the beginning of this book, you created a Pod by running `kubectl run`. It was something similar to:

```
$ kubectl run nginx --image=nginx:1.7.12
```

Under the hood, this was actually creating a `Deployment` object.

You can view this `Deployment` object by running:

```
$ kubectl get deployments nginx
NAME    DESIRED   CURRENT   UP-TO-DATE   AVAILABLE   AGE
nginx   1         1         1            1           13s
```

Deployment Internals

Let's explore how Deployments actually work. Just as we learned that ReplicaSets manage Pods, Deployments manage ReplicaSets. As with all relationships in Kubernetes, this relationship is defined by labels and a label selector. You can see the label selector by looking at the `Deployment` object:

```
$ kubectl get deployments nginx \
  -o jsonpath --template {.spec.selector.matchLabels}

map[run:nginx]
```

From this you can see that the Deployment is managing a ReplicaSet with the labels `run=nginx`. We can use this in a label selector query across ReplicaSets to find that specific ReplicaSet:

```
$ kubectl get replicasets --selector=run=nginx

NAME              DESIRED   CURRENT   READY   AGE
nginx-1128242161  1         1         1       13m
```

Now let's see the relationship between a Deployment and a ReplicaSet in action. We can resize the Deployment using the imperative `scale` command:

```
$ kubectl scale deployments nginx --replicas=2

deployment "nginx" scaled
```

Now if we list that ReplicaSet again, we should see:

```
$ kubectl get replicasets --selector=run=nginx

NAME                DESIRED   CURRENT   READY    AGE
nginx-1128242161    2         2         2        13m
```

Scaling the Deployment has also scaled the ReplicaSet it controls.

Now let's try the opposite, scaling the ReplicaSet:

```
$ kubectl scale replicasets nginx-1128242161 --replicas=1

replicaset "nginx-1128242161" scaled
```

Now get that ReplicaSet again:

```
$ kubectl get replicasets --selector=run=nginx

NAME                DESIRED   CURRENT   READY    AGE
nginx-1128242161    2         2         2        13m
```

That's odd. Despite our scaling the ReplicaSet to one replica, it still has two replicas as its desired state. What's going on? Remember, Kubernetes is an online, self-healing system. The top-level `Deployment` object is managing this ReplicaSet. When you adjust the number of replicas to one, it no longer matches the desired state of the Deployment, which has `replicas` set to 2. The Deployment controller notices this and takes action to ensure the observed state matches the desired state, in this case readjusting the number of replicas back to two.

If you ever want to manage that ReplicaSet directly, you need to delete the Deployment (remember to set `--cascade` to `false`, or else it will delete the ReplicaSet and Pods as well!).

Creating Deployments

Of course, as has been stated elsewhere, you should have a preference for declarative management of your Kubernetes configurations. This means maintaining the state of your deployments in YAML or JSON files on disk.

As a starting point, download this Deployment into a YAML file:

```
$ kubectl get deployments nginx --export -o yaml > nginx-deployment.yaml
$ kubectl replace -f nginx-deployment.yaml --save-config
```

If you look in the file, you will see something like this:

```
apiVersion: extensions/v1beta1
kind: Deployment
metadata:
  annotations:
    deployment.kubernetes.io/revision: "1"
```

```
    labels:
      run: nginx
    name: nginx
    namespace: default
  spec:
    replicas: 2
    selector:
      matchLabels:
        run: nginx
    strategy:
      rollingUpdate:
        maxSurge: 1
        maxUnavailable: 1
      type: RollingUpdate
    template:
      metadata:
        labels:
          run: nginx
      spec:
        containers:
        - image: nginx:1.7.12
          imagePullPolicy: Always
        dnsPolicy: ClusterFirst
        restartPolicy: Always
```

 A lot of read-only and default fields were removed in the preceding listing for brevity. We also need to run kubectl replace --save-config. This adds an annotation so that, when applying changes in the future, kubectl will know what the last applied configuration was for smarter merging of configs. If you always use kubectl apply, this step is only required after the first time you create a Deployment using kubectl create -f.

The Deployment spec has a very similar structure to the ReplicaSet spec. There is a Pod template, which contains a number of containers that are created for each replica managed by the Deployment. In addition to the Pod specification, there is also a strategy object:

```
...
  strategy:
    rollingUpdate:
      maxSurge: 1
      maxUnavailable: 1
    type: RollingUpdate
...
```

The strategy object dictates the different ways in which a rollout of new software can proceed. There are two different strategies supported by Deployments: Recreate and RollingUpdate.

These are discussed in detail later in this chapter.

Managing Deployments

As with all Kubernetes objects, you can get detailed information about your Deployment via the kubectl describe command:

```
$ kubectl describe deployments nginx

Name:                   nginx
Namespace:              default
CreationTimestamp:      Sat, 31 Dec 2016 09:53:32 -0800
Labels:                 run=nginx
Selector:               run=nginx
Replicas:               2 updated | 2 total | 2 available | 0 unavailable
StrategyType:           RollingUpdate
MinReadySeconds:        0
RollingUpdateStrategy:  1 max unavailable, 1 max surge
OldReplicaSets:         <none>
NewReplicaSet:          nginx-1128242161 (2/2 replicas created)
Events:
  FirstSeen   ...   Message
  ---------   ...   -------
  5m          ...   Scaled up replica set nginx-1128242161 to 1
  4m          ...   Scaled up replica set nginx-1128242161 to 2
```

In the output of describe there is a great deal of important information.

Two of the most important pieces of information in the output are OldReplicaSets and NewReplicaSet. These fields point to the ReplicaSet objects this Deployment is currently managing. If a Deployment is in the middle of a rollout, both fields will be set to a value. If a rollout is complete, OldReplicaSets will be set to <none>.

In addition to the describe command, there is also the kubectl rollout command for deployments. We will go into this command in more detail later on, but for now, you can use kubectl rollout history to obtain the history of rollouts associated with a particular Deployment. If you have a current Deployment in progress, then you can use kubectl rollout status to obtain the current status of a rollout.

Updating Deployments

Deployments are declarative objects that describe a deployed application. The two most common operations on a Deployment are scaling and application updates.

Scaling a Deployment

Although we previously showed how you could imperatively scale a Deployment using the kubectl scale command, the best practice is to manage your Deployments declaratively via the YAML files, and then use those files to update your Deployment. To scale up a Deployment, you would edit your YAML file to increase the number of replicas:

```
...
spec:
  replicas: 3
...
```

Once you have saved and committed this change, you can update the Deployment using the kubectl apply command:

```
$ kubectl apply -f nginx-deployment.yaml
```

This will update the desired state of the Deployment, causing it to increase the size of the ReplicaSet it manages, and eventually create a new Pod managed by the Deployment:

```
$ kubectl get deployments nginx
```

```
NAME    DESIRED   CURRENT   UP-TO-DATE   AVAILABLE   AGE
nginx   3         3         3            3           4m
```

Updating a Container Image

The other common use case for updating a Deployment is to roll out a new version of the software running in one or more containers. To do this, you should likewise edit the deployment YAML file, though in this case you are updating the container image, rather than the number of replicas:

```
...
    containers:
    - image: nginx:1.9.10
      imagePullPolicy: Always
...
```

We are also going to put an annotation in the template for the Deployment to record some information about the update:

```
...
spec:
  ...
  template:
    annotations:
      kubernetes.io/change-cause: "Update nginx to 1.9.10"
...
```

Make sure you add this annotation to the template and not the Deployment itself. Also, do not update the `change-cause` annotation when doing simple scaling operations. A modification of `change-cause` is a significant change to the template and will trigger a new rollout.

Again, you can use `kubectl apply` to update the Deployment:

```
$ kubectl apply -f nginx-deployment.yaml
```

After you update the Deployment it will trigger a rollout, which you can then monitor via the `kubectl rollout` command:

```
$ kubectl rollout status deployments nginx
deployment nginx successfully rolled out
```

You can see the old and new ReplicaSets managed by the deployment along with the images being used. Both the old and new ReplicaSets are kept around in case you want to roll back:

```
$ kubectl get replicasets -o wide

NAME                DESIRED   CURRENT   READY   ...   IMAGE(S)        ...
nginx-1128242161    0         0         0       ...   nginx:1.7.12    ...
nginx-1128635377    3         3         3       ...   nginx:1.9.10    ...
```

If you are in the middle of a rollout and you want to temporarily pause it for some reason (e.g., if you start seeing weird behavior in your system and you want to investigate), you can use the `pause` command:

```
$ kubectl rollout pause deployments nginx
deployment "nginx" paused
```

If, after investigation, you believe the rollout can safely proceed, you can use the `resume` command to start up where you left off:

```
$ kubectl rollout resume deployments nginx
deployment "nginx" resumed
```

Rollout History

Kubernetes Deployments maintain a history of rollouts, which can be useful both for understanding the previous state of the Deployment and to roll back to a specific version.

You can see the deployment history by running:

```
$ kubectl rollout history deployment nginx

deployments "nginx"
REVISION          CHANGE-CAUSE
```

```
1                <none>
2                Update nginx to 1.9.10
```

The revision history is given in oldest to newest order. A unique revision number is incremented for each new rollout. So far we have two: the initial deployment, the update of the image to `nginx:1.9.10`.

If you are interested in more details about a particular revision, you can add the `--revision` flag to view details about that specific revision:

```
$ kubectl rollout history deployment nginx --revision=2

deployments "nginx" with revision #2
  Labels:       pod-template-hash=2738859366
        run=nginx
  Annotations:  kubernetes.io/change-cause=Update nginx to 1.9.10
  Containers:
   nginx:
    Image:        nginx:1.9.10
    Port:
    Volume Mounts:      <none>
    Environment Variables:      <none>
  No volumes.
```

Let's do one more update for this example. Update the nginx version to 1.10.2 by modifying the container version number and updating the `change-cause` annotation. Apply it with `kubectl apply`. Our history should now have three entries:

```
$ kubectl rollout history deployment nginx

deployments "nginx"
REVISION        CHANGE-CAUSE
1               <none>
2               Update nginx to 1.9.10
3               Update nginx to 1.10.2
```

Let's say there is an issue with the latest release and you want to roll back while you investigate. You can simply undo the last rollout:

```
$ kubectl rollout undo deployments nginx
deployment "nginx" rolled back
```

The undo command works regardless of the stage of the rollout. You can undo both partially completed and fully completed rollouts. An undo of a rollout is actually simply a rollout in reverse (e.g., from *v2* to *v1*, instead of from *v1* to *v2*), and all of the same policies that control the rollout strategy apply to the undo strategy as well. You can see the Deployment object simply adjusts the desired replica counts in the managed ReplicaSets:

```
$ kubectl get replicasets -o wide

NAME                DESIRED   CURRENT   READY   ...   IMAGE(S)       ...
nginx-1128242161    0         0         0       ...   nginx:1.7.12   ...
nginx-1570155864    0         0         0       ...   nginx:1.10.2   ...
nginx-2738859366    3         3         3       ...   nginx:1.9.10   ...
```

 When using declarative files to control your production systems, you want to, as much as possible, ensure that the checked-in manifests match what is actually running in your cluster. When you do a kubectl rollout undo you are updating the production state in a way that isn't reflected in your source control.

An alternate (and perhaps preferred) way to undo a rollout is to revert your YAML file and kubectl apply the previous version. In this way your "change tracked configuration" more closely tracks what is really running in your cluster.

Let's look at our deployment history again:

```
$ kubectl rollout history deployment nginx

REVISION        CHANGE-CAUSE
1               <none>
3               Update nginx to 1.10.2
4               Update nginx to 1.9.10
```

Revision 2 is missing! It turns out that when you roll back to a previous revision, the Deployment simply reuses the template and renumbers it so that it is the latest revision. What was revision 2 before is now reordered into revision 4.

We previously saw that you can use the kubectl rollout undo command to roll back to a previous version of a deployment. Additionally, you can roll back to a specific revision in the history using the --to-revision flag:

```
$ kubectl rollout undo deployments nginx --to-revision=3
deployment "nginx" rolled back
$ kubectl rollout history deployment nginx
deployments "nginx"
REVISION        CHANGE-CAUSE
1               <none>
4               Update nginx to 1.9.10
5               Update nginx to 1.10.2
```

Again, the undo took revision 3, applied it, and renumbered it as revision 5.

Specifying a revision of 0 is a shorthand way of specifying the previous revision. In this way, kubectl rollout undo is equivalent to kubectl rollout undo --to-revision=0.

By default, the complete revision history of a Deployment is kept attached to the Deployment object itself. Over time (e.g., years) this history can grow fairly large, so it is recommended that if you have Deployments that you expect to keep around for a long time you set a maximum history size for the Deployment revision history, to limit the total size of the `Deployment` object. For example, if you do a daily update you may limit your revision history to 14, to keep a maximum of 2 weeks' worth of revisions (if you don't expect to need to roll back beyond 2 weeks).

To accomplish this, use the `revisionHistoryLimit` property in the Deployment specification:

```
...
spec:
  # We do daily rollouts, limit the revision history to two weeks of
  # releases as we don't expect to roll back beyond that.
  revisionHistoryLimit: 14
...
```

Deployment Strategies

When it comes time to change the version of software implementing your service, a Kubernetes Deployment supports two different rollout strategies:

- `Recreate`
- `RollingUpdate`

Recreate Strategy

The recreate strategy is the simpler of the two rollout strategies. It simply updates the ReplicaSet it manages to use the new image and terminates all of the Pods associated with the Deployment. The ReplicaSet notices that it no longer has any replicas, and re-creates all Pods using the new image. Once the Pods are re-created, they are running the new version.

While this strategy is fast and simple, it has one major drawback—it is potentially catastrophic, and will almost certainly result in some site downtime. Because of this, the recreate strategy should only be used for test deployments where a service is not user-facing and a small amount of downtime is acceptable.

RollingUpdate Strategy

The `RollingUpdate` strategy is the generally preferable strategy for any user-facing service. While it is slower than `Recreate`, it is also significantly more sophisticated and robust. Using `RollingUpdate`, you can roll out a new version of your service while it is still receiving user traffic, without any downtime.

As you might infer from the name, the rolling update strategy works by updating a few Pods at a time, moving incrementally until all of the Pods are running the new version of your software.

Managing multiple versions of your service

Importantly, this means that for a period of time, both the new and the old version of your service will be receiving requests and serving traffic. This has important implications for how you build your software. Namely, it is critically important that each version of your software, and all of its clients, is capable of talking interchangeably with both a slightly older and a slightly newer version of your software.

As an example of why this is important, consider the following scenario:

> You are in the middle of rolling out your frontend software; half of your servers are running version 1 and half are running version 2. A user makes an initial request to your service and downloads a client-side JavaScript library that implements your UI. This request is serviced by a version 1 server and thus the user receives the version 1 client library. This client library runs in the user's browser and makes subsequent API requests to your service. These API requests happen to be routed to a version 2 server; thus, version 1 of your JavaScript client library is talking to version 2 of your API server. If you haven't ensured compatibility between these versions, your application won't function correctly.

At first, this might seem like an extra burden. But in truth, you always had this problem; you may just not have noticed. Concretely, a user can make a request at time t just before you initiate an update. This request is serviced by a version 1 server. At t_1 you update your service to version 2. At t_2 the version 1 client code running on the user's browser runs and hits an API endpoint being operated by a version 2 server. No matter how you update your software, you have to maintain backward and forward compatibility for reliable updates. The nature of the rolling update strategy simply makes it more clear and explicit that this is something to think about.

Note that this doesn't just apply to JavaScript clients—the same thing is true of client libraries that are compiled into other services that make calls to your service. Just because you updated doesn't mean they have updated their client libraries. This sort of backward compatibility is critical to decoupling your service from systems that depend on your service. If you don't formalize your APIs and decouple yourself, you are forced to carefully manage your rollouts with all of the other systems that call into your service. This kind of tight coupling makes it extremely hard to produce the necessary agility to be able to push out new software every week, let alone every hour or every day. In the de-coupled architecture shown in Figure 12-1, the frontend is isolated from the backend via an API contract and a load balancer, whereas in the coupled architecture, a thick client compiled into the frontend is used to connect directly to the backends.

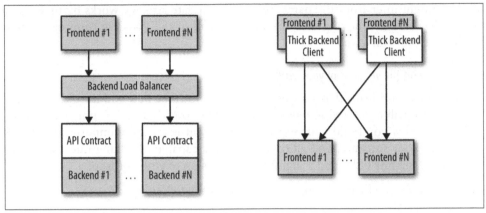

Figure 12-1. Diagrams of both de-coupled (left) and couple (right) application architectures

Configuring a rolling update

`RollingUpdate` is a fairly generic strategy; it can be used to update a variety of applications in a variety of settings. Consequently, the rolling update itself is quite configurable; you can tune its behavior to suit your particular needs. There are two parameters you can use to tune the rolling update behavior: `maxUnavailable` and `max Surge`.

The `maxUnavailable` parameter sets the maximum number of Pods that can be unavailable during a rolling update. It can either be set to an absolute number (e.g., 3 meaning a maximum of three Pods can be unavailable) or to a percentage (e.g., `20%` meaning a maximum of 20% of the desired number of replicas can be unavailable).

Generally speaking, using a percentage is a good approach for most services, since the value is correctly applicable regardless of the desired number of replicas in the Deployment. However, there are times when you may want to use an absolute number (e.g., limiting the maximum unavailable pods to one).

At its core, the `maxUnavailable` parameter helps tune how quickly a rolling update proceeds. For example, if you set `maxUnavailable` to `50%`, then the rolling update will immediately scale the old ReplicaSet down to 50% of its original size. If you have four replicas, it will scale it down to two replicas. The rolling update will then replace the removed pods by scaling the new ReplicaSet up to two replicas, for a total of four replicas (two old, two new). It will then scale the old ReplicaSet down to zero replicas, for a total size of two new replicas. Finally, it will scale the new ReplicaSet up to four replicas, completing the rollout. Thus, with `maxUnavailable` set to `50%`, our rollout completes in four steps, but with only 50% of our service capacity at times.

Consider instead what happens if we set `maxUnavailable` to `25%`. In this situation, each step is only performed with a single replica at a time and thus it takes twice as many steps for the rollout to complete, but availability only drops to a minimum of 75% during the rollout. This illustrates how `maxUnavailable` allows us to trade rollout speed for availability.

The observant among you will note that the recreate strategy is actually identical to the rolling update strategy with `maxUnavaila ble` set to `100%`.

Using reduced capacity to achieve a successful rollout is useful either when your service has cyclical traffic patterns (e.g., much less traffic at night) or when you have limited resources, so scaling to larger than the current maximum number of replicas isn't possible.

However, there are situations where you don't want to fall below 100% capacity, but you are willing to temporarily use additional resources in order to perform a rollout. In these situations, you can set the `maxUnavailable` parameter to `0%`, and instead control the rollout using the `maxSurge` parameter. Like `maxUnavailable`, `maxSurge` can be specified either as a specific number or a percentage.

The `maxSurge` parameter controls how many extra resources can be created to achieve a rollout. To illustrate how this works, imagine we have a service with 10 replicas. We set `maxUnavailable` to `0` and `maxSurge` to `20%`. The first thing the rollout will do is scale the new ReplicaSet up to 2 replicas, for a total of 12 (120%) in the service. It will then scale the old ReplicaSet down to 8 replicas, for a total of 10 (8 old, 2 new) in the service. This process proceeds until the rollout is complete. At any time, the capacity of the service is guaranteed to be at least 100% and the maximum extra resources used for the rollout are limited to an additional 20% of all resources.

Setting `maxSurge` to `100%` is equivalent to a blue/green deployment. The Deployment controller first scales the new version up to 100% of the old version. Once the new version is healthy, it immediately scales the old version down to 0%.

Slowing Rollouts to Ensure Service Health

The purpose of a staged rollout is to ensure that the rollout results in a healthy, stable service running the new software version. To do this, the Deployment controller always waits until a Pod reports that it is ready before moving on to updating the next Pod.

 The Deployment controller examines the Pod's status as determined by its readiness checks. Readiness checks are part of the Pod's health probes, and they are described in detail in Chapter 5. If you want to use Deployments to reliably roll out your software, you *have* to specify readiness health checks for the containers in your Pod. Without these checks the Deployment controller is running blind.

Sometimes, however, simply noticing that a Pod has become ready doesn't give you sufficient confidence that the Pod actually is behaving correctly. Some error conditions only occur after a period of time. For example, you could have a serious memory leak that still takes a few minutes to show up, or you could have a bug that is only triggered by 1% of all requests. In most real-world scenarios, you want to wait a period of time to have high confidence that the new version is operating correctly before you move on to updating the next Pod.

For deployments, this time to wait is defined by the `minReadySeconds` parameter:

```
...
spec:
  minReadySeconds: 60
...
```

Setting `minReadySeconds` to 60 indicates that the Deployment must wait for 60 seconds *after* seeing a Pod become healthy before moving on to updating the next Pod.

In addition to waiting a period of time for a Pod to become healthy, you also want to set a timeout that limits how long the system will wait. Suppose, for example, the new version of your service has a bug and immediately deadlocks. It will never become ready, and in the absence of a timeout, the Deployment controller will stall your rollout forever.

The correct behavior in such a situation is to time out the rollout. This in turn marks the rollout as failed. This failure status can be used to trigger alerting that can indicate to an operator that there is a problem with the rollout.

At first blush, timing out a rollout might seem like a unnecessary complication. However, increasingly, things like rollouts are being triggered by fully automated systems with little to no human involvement. In such a situation, timing out becomes a critical exception, which can either trigger an automated rollback of the release or create a ticket/event that triggers human intervention.

To set the timeout period, the Deployment parameter `progressDeadlineSeconds` is used:

```
...
spec:
  progressDeadlineSeconds: 600
```

This example sets the progress deadline to 10 minutes. If any particular stage in the rollout fails to progress in 10 minutes, then the Deployment is marked as failed, and all attempts to move the Deployment forward are halted.

It is important to note that this timeout is given in terms of Deployment *progress*, not the overall length of a Deployment. In this context progress is defined as any time the deployment creates or deletes a Pod. When that happens, the timeout clock is reset to zero. Figure 12-2 is an illustration of the deployment lifecycle.

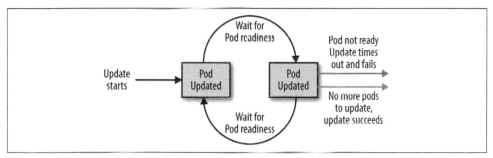

Figure 12-2. The Kubernetes Deployment lifecycle

Deleting a Deployment

If you ever want to delete a deployment, you can do it either with the imperative command:

```
$ kubectl delete deployments nginx
```

or using the declarative YAML file we created earlier:

```
$ kubectl delete -f nginx-deployment.yaml
```

In either case, by default, deleting a Deployment deletes the entire service. It will delete not just the Deployment, but also any ReplicaSets being managed by the

Deployment, as well as any Pods being managed by the ReplicaSets. As with Replica-Sets, if this is not the desired behavior, you can use the `--cascade=false` flag to exclusively delete the `Deployment` object.

Summary

At the end of the day, the primary goal of Kubernetes is to make it easy for you to build and deploy reliable distributed systems. This means not just instantiating the application once, but managing the regularly scheduled rollout of new versions of that software service. Deployments are a critical piece of reliable rollouts and rollout management for your services.

## CHAPTER 13

Integrating Storage Solutions and Kubernetes

In many cases decoupling state from applications and building your microservices to be as stateless as possible results in maximally reliable, manageable systems.

However, nearly every system that has any complexity has state in the system somewhere, from the records in a database to the index shards that serve results for a web search engine. At some point you have to have data stored somewhere.

Integrating this data with containers and container orchestration solutions is often the most complicated aspect of building a distributed system. This complexity largely stems from the fact that the move to containerized architectures is also a move toward decoupled, immutable, and declarative application development. These patterns are relatively easy to apply to stateless web applications, but even "cloud-native" storage solutions like Cassandra or MongoDB involve some sort of manual or imperative steps to set up a reliable, replicated solution.

As an example of this, consider setting up a ReplicaSet in MongoDB, which involves deploying the Mongo daemon and then running an imperative command to identify the leader, as well as the participants in the Mongo cluster. Of course, these steps can be scripted, but in a containerized world it is difficult to see how to integrate such commands into a deployment. Likewise, even getting DNS-resolvable names for individual containers in a replicated set of containers is challenging.

Additional complexity comes from the fact that there is data gravity. Most containerized systems aren't built in a vacuum; they are usually adapted from existing systems deployed onto VMs, and these systems likely include data that has to be imported or migrated.

Finally, evolution to the cloud means that many times storage is actually an externalized cloud service, and in that context it can never really exist inside of the Kubernetes cluster.

This chapter covers a variety of approaches for integrating storage into containerized microservices in Kubernetes. First, we cover how to import existing external storage solutions (either cloud services or running on VMs) into Kubernetes. Next, we explore how to run reliable singletons inside of Kubernetes that enable you to have an environment that largely matches the VMs where you previously deployed storage solutions. Finally we cover StatefulSets, which are still under development but represent the future of stateful workloads in Kubernetes.

Importing External Services

In many cases, you have an existing machine running in your network that has some sort of database running on it. In this situation you may not want to immediately move that database into containers and Kubernetes. Perhaps it is run by a different team, or you are doing a gradual move, or the task of migrating the data is simply more trouble than it's worth.

Regardless of the reasons for staying put, this legacy server and service are not going to move into Kubernetes, but nonetheless it is still worthwhile to represent this server in Kubernetes. When you do this, you get to take advantage of all of the built-in naming and service discovery primitives provided by Kubernetes. Additionally, this enables you to configure all your applications so that it looks like the database that is running on a machine somewhere is actually a Kubernetes service. This means that it is trivial to replace it with a database that is a Kubernetes service. For example, in production, you may rely on your legacy database that is running on a machine, but for continuous testing you may deploy a test database as a transient container. Since it is created and destroyed for each test run, data persistence isn't important in the continuous testing case. Representing both databases as Kubernetes services enables you to maintain identical configurations in both testing and production. High fidelity between test and production ensures that passing tests will lead to successful deployment in production.

To see concretely how you maintain high fidelity between development and production, remember that all Kubernetes objects are deployed into *namespaces*. Imagine that we have test and product namespaces defined. The test service is imported using an object like:

```
kind: Service
metadata:
  name: my-database
  # note 'test' namespace here
```

```
  namespace: test
...
```

The production service looks the same, except it uses a different namespace:

```
kind: Service
metadata:
  name: my-database
  # note 'prod' namespace here
  namespace: prod
...
```

When you deploy a Pod into the `test` namespace and it looks up the service named `my-database`, it will receive a pointer to `my-database.test.svc.cluster.internal`, which in turn points to the test database. In contrast, when a Pod deployed in the `prod` namespace looks up the same name (`my-database`) it will receive a pointer to `my-database.prod.svc.cluster.internal`, which is the production database. Thus, the same service name, in two different namespaces, resolves to two different services. For more details on how this works, see Chapter 7.

 The following techniques all use database or other storage services, but these approaches can be used equally well with other services that aren't running inside your Kubernetes cluster.

Services Without Selectors

When we first introduced services, we talked at length about label queries and how they were used to identify the dynamic set of Pods that were the backends for a particular service. With external services, however, there is no such label query. Instead, you generally have a DNS name that points to the specific server running the database. For our example, let's assume that this server is named `database.company.com`. To import this external database service into Kubernetes, we start by creating a service without a Pod selector that references the DNS name of the database server (Example 13-1).

Example 13-1. dns-service.yaml

```
kind: Service
apiVersion: v1
metadata:
  name: external-database
spec:
  type: ExternalName
  externalName: "database.company.com
```

When a typical Kubernetes service is created, an IP address is also created and the Kubernetes DNS service is populated with an A record that points to that IP address. When you create a service of type ExternalName, the Kubernetes DNS service is instead populated with a CNAME record that points to the external name you specified (database.company.com in this case). When an application in the cluster does a DNS lookup for the hostname external-database.svc.default.cluster, the DNS protocol aliases that name to "database.company.com." This then resolves to the IP address of your external database server. In this way, all containers in Kubernetes believe that they are talking to a service that is backed with other containers, when in fact they are being redirected to the external database.

Note that this is not restricted to databases you are running on your own infrastructure. Many cloud databases and other services provide you with a DNS name to use when accessing the database (e.g., my-database.databases.cloudprovider.com). You can use this DNS name as the externalName. This imports the cloud-provided database into the namespace of your Kubernetes cluster.

Sometimes, however, you don't have a DNS address for an external database service, just an IP address. In such cases, it is still possible to import this server as a Kubernetes service, but the operation is a little different. First, you create a Service without a label selector, but also without the ExternalName type we used before (Example 13-2).

Example 13-2. external-ip-service.yaml

```
kind: Service
apiVersion: v1
metadata:
  name: external-ip-database
```

At this point, Kubernetes will allocate a virtual IP address for this service and populate an A record for it. However, because there is no selector for the service, there will be no endpoints populated for the load balancer to redirect traffic to.

Given that this is an external service, the user is responsible for populating the endpoints manually with an Endpoints resource (Example 13-3).

Example 13-3. external-ip-endpoints.yaml

```
kind: Endpoints
apiVersion: v1
metadata:
  name: external-ip-database
subsets:
  - addresses:
    - ip: 192.168.0.1
```

```
ports:
- port: 3306
```

If you have more than one IP address for redundancy, you can repeat them in the addresses array. Once the endpoints are populated, the load balancer will start redirecting traffic from your Kubernetes service to the IP address endpoint(s).

 Because the user has assumed responsibility for keeping the IP address of the server up to date, you need to either ensure that it never changes or make sure that some automated process updates the Endpoints record.

Limitations of External Services: Health Checking

External services in Kubernetes have one significant restriction: they do not perform any health checking. The user is responsible for ensuring that the endpoint or DNS name supplied to Kubernetes is as reliable as necessary for the application.

Running Reliable Singletons

The challenge of running storage solutions in Kubernetes is often that primitives like ReplicaSet expect that every container is identical and replaceable, but for most storage solutions this isn't the case. One option to address this is to use Kubernetes primitives, but not attempt to replicate the storage. Instead, simply run a single Pod that runs the database or other storage solution. In this way the challenges of running replicated storage in Kubernetes don't occur, since there is no replication.

At first blush, this might seem to run counter to the principles of building reliable distributed systems, but in general, it is no less reliable than running your database or storage infrastructure on a single virtual or physical machine, which is how many people currently have built their systems. Indeed, in reality, if you structure the system properly the only thing you are sacrificing is potential downtime for upgrades or in case of machine failure. While for large-scale or mission-critical systems this may not be acceptable, for many smaller-scale applications this kind of limited downtime is a reasonable trade-off for the reduced complexity. If this is not true for you, feel free to skip this section and either import existing services as described in the previous section, or move on to Kubernetes-native StatefulSets, described in the following section. For everyone else, we'll review how to build reliable singletons for data storage.

Running a MySQL Singleton

In this section, we'll describe how to run a reliable singleton instance of the MySQL database as a Pod in Kubernetes, and how to expose that singleton to other applications in the cluster.

To do this, we are going to create three basic objects:

- A persistent volume to manage the lifespan of the on-disk storage independently from the lifespan of the running MySQL application
- A MySQL Pod that will run the MySQL application
- A service that will expose this Pod to other containers in the cluster

In Chapter 5 we described persistent volumes, but a quick review makes sense. A persistent volume is a storage location that has a lifetime independent of any Pod or container. This is very useful in the case of persistent storage solutions where the on-disk representation of a database should survive even if the containers running the database application crash, or move to different machines. If the application moves to a different machine, the volume should move with it, and data should be preserved. Separating the data storage out as a persistent volume makes this possible. To begin, we'll create a persistent volume for our MySQL database to use.

This example uses NFS for maximum portability, but Kubernetes supports many different persistent volume drive types. For example, there are persistent volume drivers for all major public cloud providers, as well as many private cloud providers. To use these solutions, simply replace `nfs` with the appropriate cloud provider volume type (e.g., `azure`, `awsElasticBlockStore`, or `gcePersistentDisk`). In all cases, this change is all you need. Kubernetes knows how to create the appropriate storage disk in the respective cloud provider. This is a great example of how Kubernetes simplifies the development of reliable distributed systems.

Here's the example persistent volume object (Example 13-4).

Example 13-4. nfs-volume.yaml

```
apiVersion: v1
kind: PersistentVolume
metadata:
  name: database
  labels:
    volume: my-volume
spec:
  capacity:
    storage: 1Gi
  nfs:
```

```
    server: 192.168.0.1
    path: "/exports"
```

This defines an NFS persistent volume object with 1 GB of storage space.

We can create this persistent volume as usual with:

```
$ kubectl apply -f nfs-volume.yaml
```

Now that we have a persistent volume created, we need to claim that persistent volume for our Pod. We do this with a `PersistentVolumeClaim` object (Example 13-5).

Example 13-5. nfs-volume-claim.yaml

```
kind: PersistentVolumeClaim
apiVersion: v1
metadata:
  name: database
spec:
  resources:
    requests:
      storage: 1Gi
  selector:
    matchLabels:
      volume: my-volume
```

The `selector` field uses labels to find the matching volume we defined previously.

This kind of indirection may seem overly complicated, but it has a purpose—it serves to isolate our Pod definition from our storage definition. You can declare volumes directly inside a Pod specification, but this locks that Pod specification to a particular volume provider (e.g., a specific public or private cloud). By using volume claims, you can keep your Pod specifications cloud-agnostic; simply create different volumes, specific to the cloud, and use a `PersistentVolumeClaim` to bind them together.

Now that we've claimed our volume, we can use a ReplicaSet to construct our singleton Pod. It might seem odd that we are using a ReplicaSet to manage a single Pod, but it is necessary for reliability. Remember that once scheduled to a machine, a bare Pod is bound to that machine forever. If the machine fails, then any Pods that are on that machine that are not being managed by a higher-level controller like a ReplicaSet vanish along with the machine and are not rescheduled elsewhere. Consequently, to ensure that our database Pod is rescheduled in the presence of machine failures, we use the higher-level ReplicaSet controller, with a replica size of one, to manage our database (Example 13-6).

Example 13-6. mysql-replicaset.yaml

```yaml
apiVersion: extensions/v1beta1
kind: ReplicaSet
metadata:
  name: mysql
  # labels so that we can bind a Service to this Pod
  labels:
    app: mysql
spec:
  replicas: 1
  selector:
    matchLabels:
      app: mysql
  template:
    metadata:
      labels:
        app: mysql
    spec:
      containers:
      - name: database
        image: mysql
        resources:
          requests:
            cpu: 1
            memory: 2Gi
        env:
        # Environment variables are not a best practice for security,
        # but we're using them here for brevity in the example.
        # See Chapter 11 for better options.
        - name: MYSQL_ROOT_PASSWORD
          value: some-password-here
        livenessProbe:
          tcpSocket:
            port: 3306
        ports:
        - containerPort: 3306
        volumeMounts:
          - name: database
            # /var/lib/mysql is where MySQL stores its databases
            mountPath: "/var/lib/mysql"
      volumes:
      - name: database
        persistentVolumeClaim:
          claimName: database
```

Once we create the `ReplicaSet` it will in turn create a Pod running MySQL using the persistent disk we originally created. The final step is to expose this as a Kubernetes service (Example 13-7).

Example 13-7. mysql-service.yaml

```
apiVersion: v1
kind: Service
metadata:
  name: mysql
spec:
  ports:
  - port: 3306
    protocol: TCP
  selector:
    app: mysql
```

Now we have a reliable singleton MySQL instance running in our cluster and exposed as a service named `mysql`, which we can access at the full domain name `mysql.svc.default.cluster`.

Similar instructions can be used for a variety of data stores, and if your needs are simple and you can survive limited downtime in the face of a machine failure or a need to upgrade the database software, a reliable singleton may be the right approach to storage for your application.

Dynamic Volume Provisioning

Many clusters also include *dynamic volume provisioning*. With dynamic volume provisioning, the cluster operator creates one or more `StorageClass` objects. Here's a default storage class that automatically provisions disk objects on the Microsoft Azure platform (Example 13-8).

Example 13-8. storageclass.yaml

```
apiVersion: storage.k8s.io/v1beta1
kind: StorageClass
metadata:
  name: default
  annotations:
    storageclass.beta.kubernetes.io/is-default-class: "true"
  labels:
    kubernetes.io/cluster-service: "true"
provisioner: kubernetes.io/azure-disk
```

Once a storage class has been created for a cluster, you can refer to this storage class in your persistent volume claim, rather than referring to any specific persistent volume. When the dynamic provisioner sees this storage claim, it uses the appropriate volume driver to create the volume and bind it to your persistent volume claim.

Here's an example of a `PersistentVolumeClaim` that uses the `default` storage class we just defined to claim a newly created persistent volume (Example 13-9).

Example 13-9. dynamic-volume-claim.yaml

```
kind: PersistentVolumeClaim
apiVersion: v1
metadata:
  name: my-claim
  annotations:
    volume.beta.kubernetes.io/storage-class: default
spec:
  accessModes:
  - ReadWriteOnce
  resources:
    requests:
      storage: 10Gi
```

The `volume.beta.kubernetes.io/storage-class` annotation is what links this claim back up to the storage class we created.

Persistent volumes are great for traditional applications that require storage, but if you need to develop high-availability, scalable storage in a Kubernetes-native fashion, the newly released StatefulSet object can be used. With this in mind, we'll describe how to deploy MongoDB using StatefulSets in the next section.

Kubernetes-Native Storage with StatefulSets

When Kubernetes was first developed, there was a heavy emphasis on homogeneity for all replicas in a replicated set. In this design, no replica had an individual identity or configuration. It was up to the individual application developer to determine a design that could establish this identity for the application.

While this approach provides a great deal of isolation for the orchestration system, it also makes it quite difficult to develop stateful applications. After significant input from the community and a great deal of experimentation with various existing stateful applications, StatefulSets were introduced into Kubernetes in version 1.5.

 Because StatefulSets are a beta feature, it's possible that the API will change before it becomes an official Kubernetes API. The Stateful-Set API has had a lot of input and is generally considered fairly stable, but the beta status should be considered before taking on StatefulSets. In many cases the previously outlined patterns for stateful applications may serve you better in the near term.

Properties of StatefulSets

StatefulSets are replicated groups of Pods similar to ReplicaSets, but unlike a Replica-Set, they have certain unique properties:

- Each replica gets a persistent hostname with a unique index (e.g., `database-0`, `database-1`, etc.).

- Each replica is created in order from lowest to highest index, and creation will block until the Pod at the previous index is healthy and available. This also applies to scaling up.

- When deleted, each replica will be deleted in order from highest to lowest. This also applies to scaling down the number of replicas.

Manually Replicated MongoDB with StatefulSets

In this section, we'll deploy a replicated MongoDB cluster. For now, the replication setup itself will be done manually to give you a feel for how StatefulSets work. Eventually we will automate this setup as well.

To start, we'll create a replicated set of three MongoDB Pods using a StatefulSet object (Example 13-10).

Example 13-10. mongo-simple.yaml

```
apiVersion: apps/v1beta1
kind: StatefulSet
metadata:
  name: mongo
spec:
  serviceName: "mongo"
  replicas: 3
  template:
    metadata:
      labels:
        app: mongo
    spec:
      containers:
      - name: mongodb
        image: mongo:3.4.1
        command:
        - mongod
        - --replSet
        - rs0
        ports:
        - containerPort: 27017
          name: peer
```

As you can see, the definition is similar to the ReplicaSet definition from previous sections. The only changes are the `apiVersion` and `kind` fields. Create the StatefulSet:

```
$ kubectl apply -f mongo-simple.yaml
```

Once created, the differences between a ReplicaSet and a StatefulSet become apparent. Run `kubectl get pods` and you will likely see:

```
NAME      READY   STATUS             RESTARTS   AGE
mongo-0   1/1     Running            0          1m
mongo-1   0/1     ContainerCreating  0          10s
```

There are two important differences between this and what you would see with a ReplicaSet. The first is that each replicated Pod has a numeric index (0, 1, ...), instead of the random suffix that is added by the ReplicaSet controller. The second is that the Pods are being slowly created in order, not all at once as they would be with a ReplicaSet.

Once the StatefulSet is created, we also need to create a "headless" service to manage the DNS entries for the StatefulSet. In Kubernetes a service is called "headless" if it doesn't have a cluster virtual IP address. Since with StatefulSets each Pod has a unique identity, it doesn't really make sense to have a load-balancing IP address for the replicated service. You can create a headless service using `clusterIP: None` in the service specification (Example 13-11).

Example 13-11. mongo-service.yaml

```yaml
apiVersion: v1
kind: Service
metadata:
  name: mongo
spec:
  ports:
  - port: 27017
    name: peer
  clusterIP: None
  selector:
    app: mongo
```

Once you create that service, there are usually four DNS entries that are populated. As usual, `mongo.default.svc.cluster.local` is created, but unlike with a standard service, doing a DNS lookup on this hostname provides all the addresses in the StatefulSet. In addition, entries are created for `mongo-0.mongo.default.svc.cluster.local` as well as `mongo-1.mongo` and `mongo-2.mongo`. Each of these resolves to the specific IP address of the replica index in the StatefulSet. Thus, with StatefulSets you get well-defined, persistent names for each replica in the set. This is often very useful when you are configuring a replicated storage solution. You can see these DNS entries in action by running commands in one of the Mongo replicas:

```
$ kubectl exec mongo-0 bash ping mongo-1.mongo
```

Next, we're going to manually set up Mongo replication using these per-Pod hostnames.

We'll choose `mongo-0.mongo` to be our initial primary. Run the `mongo` tool in that Pod:

```
$ kubectl exec -it mongo-0 mongo
> rs.initiate( {
  _id: "rs0",
  members:[ { _id: 0, host: "mongo-0.mongo:27017" } ]
});
OK
```

This command tells `mongodb` to initiate the ReplicaSet `rs0` with `mongo-0.mongo` as the primary replica.

 The `rs0` name is arbitrary. You can use whatever you'd like, but you'll need to change it in the *mongo.yaml* StatefulSet definition as well.

Once you have initiated the Mongo ReplicaSet, you can add the remaining replicas by running the following commands in the `mongo` tool on the `mongo-0.mongo` Pod:

```
$ kubectl exec -it mongo-0 mongo
> rs.add("mongo-1.mongo:27017");
> rs.add("mongo-2.mongo:27017");
```

As you can see, we are using the replica-specific DNS names to add them as replicas in our Mongo cluster. At this point, we're done. Our replicated MongoDB is up and running. But it's really not as automated as we'd like it to be. In the next section, we'll see how to use scripts to automate the setup.

Automating MongoDB Cluster Creation

To automate the deployment of our StatefulSet-based MongoDB cluster, we're going to add an additional container to our Pods to perform the initialization.

To configure this Pod without having to build a new Docker image, we're going to use a ConfigMap to add a script into the existing MongoDB image. Here's the container we're adding:

```
    ...
        - name: init-mongo
          image: mongo:3.4.1
          command:
          - bash
          - /config/init.sh
          volumeMounts:
          - name: config
            mountPath: /config
        volumes:
        - name: config
```

```
        configMap:
            name: "mongo-init"
```

Note that it is mounting a ConfigMap volume whose name is `mongo-init`. This ConfigMap holds a script that performs our initialization. First, the script determines whether it is running on `mongo-0` or not. If it is on `mongo-0`, it creates the ReplicaSet using the same command we ran imperatively previously. If it is on a different Mongo replica, it waits until the ReplicaSet exists, and then it registers itself as a member of that ReplicaSet.

Example 13-12 has the complete ConfigMap object.

Example 13-12. mongo-configmap.yaml

```
apiVersion: v1
kind: ConfigMap
metadata:
  name: mongo-init
data:
  init.sh: |
    #!/bin/bash

    # Need to wait for the readiness health check to pass so that the
    # mongo names resolve. This is kind of wonky.
    until ping -c 1 ${HOSTNAME}.mongo; do
      echo "waiting for DNS (${HOSTNAME}.mongo)..."
      sleep 2
    done

    until /usr/bin/mongo --eval 'printjson(db.serverStatus())'; do
      echo "connecting to local mongo..."
      sleep 2
    done
    echo "connected to local."

    HOST=mongo-0.mongo:27017

    until /usr/bin/mongo --host=${HOST} --eval 'printjson(db.serverStatus())'; do
      echo "connecting to remote mongo..."
      sleep 2
    done
    echo "connected to remote."

    if [[ "${HOSTNAME}" != 'mongo-0' ]]; then
      until /usr/bin/mongo --host=${HOST} --eval="printjson(rs.status())" \
            | grep -v "no replset config has been received"; do
        echo "waiting for replication set initialization"
        sleep 2
      done
      echo "adding self to mongo-0"
      /usr/bin/mongo --host=${HOST} \
```

```
    --eval="printjson(rs.add('${HOSTNAME}.mongo'))"
  fi

  if [[ "${HOSTNAME}" == 'mongo-0' ]]; then
    echo "initializing replica set"
    /usr/bin/mongo --eval="printjson(rs.initiate(\
        {'_id': 'rs0', 'members': [{'_id': 0, \
        'host': 'mongo-0.mongo:27017'}]}))"
  fi
  echo "initialized"

  while true; do
    sleep 3600
  done
```

 This script currently sleeps forever after initializing the cluster. Every container in a Pod has to have the same RestartPolicy. Since we want our main Mongo container to be restarted, we need to have our initialization container run forever too, or else Kubernetes might think our Mongo Pod is unhealthy.

Putting it all together, here is the complete StatefulSet that uses the ConfigMap in Example 13-13.

Example 13-13. mongo.yaml

```
apiVersion: apps/v1beta1
kind: StatefulSet
metadata:
  name: mongo
spec:
  serviceName: "mongo"
  replicas: 3
  template:
    metadata:
      labels:
        app: mongo
    spec:
      containers:
      - name: mongodb
        image: mongo:3.4.1
        command:
        - mongod
        - --replSet
        - rs0
        ports:
        - containerPort: 27017
          name: web
      # This container initializes the mongodb server, then sleeps.
      - name: init-mongo
```

```
    image: mongo:3.4.1
    command:
    - bash
    - /config/init.sh
    volumeMounts:
    - name: config
      mountPath: /config
volumes:
- name: config
  configMap:
    name: "mongo-init"
```

Given all of these files, you can create a Mongo cluster with:

```
$ kubectl apply -f mongo-config-map.yaml
$ kubectl apply -f mongo-service.yaml
$ kubectl apply -f mongo.yaml
```

Or if you want, you can combine them all into a single YAML file where the individual objects are separated by `---`. Ensure that you keep the same ordering, since the StatefulSet definition relies on the ConfigMap definition existing.

Persistent Volumes and StatefulSets

For persistent storage, you need to mount a persistent volume into the */data/db* directory. In the Pod template, you need to update it to mount a persistent volume claim to that directory:

```
...
        volumeMounts:
        - name: database
          mountPath: /data/db
```

While this approach is similar to the one we saw with reliable singletons, because the StatefulSet replicates more than one Pod you cannot simply reference a persistent volume claim. Instead, you need to add a *persistent volume claim template*. You can think of the claim template as being identical to the Pod template, but instead of creating Pods, it creates volume claims. You need to add the following onto the bottom of your StatefulSet definition:

```
volumeClaimTemplates:
- metadata:
    name: database
    annotations:
      volume.alpha.kubernetes.io/storage-class: anything
  spec:
    accessModes: [ "ReadWriteOnce" ]
    resources:
      requests:
        storage: 100Gi
```

When you add a volume claim template to a StatefulSet definition, each time the StatefulSet controller creates a Pod that is part of the StatefulSet it will create a persistent volume claim based on this template as part of that Pod.

 In order for these replicated persistent volumes to work correctly, you either need to have autoprovisioning set up for persistent volumes, or you need to prepopulate a collection of persistent volume objects for the StatefulSet controller to draw from. If there are no claims that can be created, the StatefulSet controller will not be able to create the corresponding Pods.

One Final Thing: Readiness Probes

The final piece in productionizing our MongoDB cluster is to add liveness checks to our Mongo-serving containers. As we learned in "Health Checks" on page 45, the liveness probe is used to determine if a container is operating correctly. For the liveness checks, we can use the mongo tool itself by adding the following to the Pod template in the StatefulSet object:

```
...
livenessProbe:
  exec:
    command:
      - /usr/bin/mongo
      - --eval
      - db.serverStatus()
    initialDelaySeconds: 10
    timeoutSeconds: 10
...
```

Summary

Once we have combined StatefulSets, persistent volume claims, and liveness probing, we have a hardened, scalable cloud-native MongoDB installation running on Kubernetes. While this example dealt with MongoDB, the steps for creating StatefulSets to manage other storage solutions are quite similar and similar patterns can be followed.

## CHAPTER 14

Deploying Real-World Applications

The previous chapters described a variety of API objects that are available in a Kubernetes cluster and ways in which those objects can best be used to construct reliable distributed systems. However, none of the preceding chapters really discussed how you might use the objects in practice to deploy a complete, real world application. That is the focus of this chapter.

We'll take a look at three real-world applications:

- Parse, an open source API server for mobile applications
- Ghost, a blogging and content management platform
- Redis, a lightweight, performant key/value store

These complete examples should give you a better idea of how to structure your own deployments using Kubernetes.

Parse

The Parse server (*https://parse.com*) is a cloud API dedicated to providing easy-to-use storage for mobile applications. It provides a variety of different client libraries that make it easy to integrate with Android, iOS, and other mobile platforms. Parse was purchased by Facebook in 2013 and subsequently shut down. Fortunately for us, a compatible server was open sourced by the core Parse team and is available for us to use. This section describes how to set up Parse in Kubernetes.

Prerequisites

Parse uses MongoDB cluster for its storage. Chapter 13 described how to set up a replicated MongoDB using Kubernetes StatefulSets. This section assumes you have a three-replica Mongo cluster running in Kubernetes with the names `mongo-0.mongo`, `mongo-1.mongo`, and `mongo-2.mongo`.

These instructions also assume that you have a Docker login; if you don't have one, you can get one for free at *https://docker.com*.

Finally, we assume you have a Kubernetes cluster deployed and the `kubectl` tool properly configured.

Building the parse-server

The open source `parse-server` comes with a *Dockerfile* by default, for easy containerization. First, clone the Parse repository:

```
$ git clone https://github.com/ParsePlatform/parse-server
```

Then move into that directory and build the image:

```
$ cd parse-server
$ docker build -t ${DOCKER_USER}/parse-server .
```

Finally, push that image up to the Docker hub:

```
$ docker push ${DOCKER_USER}/parse-server
```

Deploying the parse-server

Once you have the container image built, deploying the `parse-server` into your cluster is fairly straightforward. Parse looks for three environment variables when being configured:

`APPLICATION_ID`
    An identifier for authorizing your application

`MASTER_KEY`
    An identifier that authorizes the master (root) user

`DATABASE_URI`
    The URI for your MongoDB cluster

Putting this all together, you can deploy Parse as a Kubernetes Deployment using the YAML file in Example 14-1.

Example 14-1. parse.yaml

```
apiVersion: extensions/v1beta1
kind: Deployment
metadata:
  name: parse-server
  namespace: default
```

```
spec:
  replicas: 1
  template:
    metadata:
      labels:
        run: parse-server
    spec:
      containers:
      - name: parse-server
        image: ${DOCKER_USER}/parse-server
        env:
        - name: DATABASE_URI
          value: "mongodb://mongo-0.mongo:27017,\
            mongo-1.mongo:27017,mongo-2.mongo\
            :27017/dev?replicaset=rs0"
        - name: APP_ID
          value: my-app-id
        - name: MASTER_KEY
          value: my-master-key
```

Testing Parse

To test your deployment, you need to expose it as a Kubernetes service. You can do that using the service definition in Example 14-2.

Example 14-2. parse-service.yaml

```
apiVersion: v1
kind: Service
metadata:
  name: parse-server
  namespace: default
spec:
  ports:
  - port: 1337
    protocol: TCP
    targetPort: 1337
  selector:
    run: parse-server
```

Now your Parse server is up and running and ready to receive requests from your mobile applications. Of course, in any real application you are likely going to want to secure the connection with HTTPS. You can see the parse-server GitHub page (*https://github.com/parse-community/parse-server*) for more details on such a configuration.

Ghost

Ghost is a popular blogging engine with a clean interface written in JavaScript. It can either use a file-based SQLite database or MySQL for storage.

Configuring Ghost

Ghost is configured with a simple JavaScript file that describes the server. We will store this file as a configuration map. A simple development configuration for Ghost looks like Example 14-3.

Example 14-3. ghost-config.js

```
var path = require('path'),
    config;

config = {
    development: {
        url: 'http://localhost:2368',
        database: {
            client: 'sqlite3',
            connection: {
                filename: path.join(process.env.GHOST_CONTENT,
                                    '/data/ghost-dev.db')
            },
            debug: false
        },
        server: {
            host: '0.0.0.0',
            port: '2368'
        },
        paths: {
            contentPath: path.join(process.env.GHOST_CONTENT, '/')
        }
    }
};

module.exports = config;
```

Once you have this configuration file saved to *config.js*, you can create a Kubernetes ConfigMap object using:

```
$ kubectl apply cm --from-file ghost-config.js ghost-config
```

This creates a ConfigMap that is named `ghost-config`. As with the Parse example, we will mount this configuration file as a volume inside of our container. We will deploy Ghost as a `Deployment` object, which defines this volume mount as part of the Pod template (Example 14-4).

Example 14-4. ghost.yaml

```
apiVersion: extensions/v1beta1
kind: Deployment
metadata:
  name: ghost
spec:
  replicas: 1
  selector:
    matchLabels:
      run: ghost
  template:
    metadata:
      labels:
        run: ghost
    spec:
      containers:
      - image: ghost
        name: ghost
        command:
        - sh
        - -c
        - cp /ghost-config/config.js /var/lib/ghost/config.js
          && /entrypoint.sh npm start
        volumeMounts:
        - mountPath: /ghost-config
          name: config
      volumes:
      - name: config
        configMap:
          defaultMode: 420
          name: ghost-config
```

One thing to note here is that we are copying the *config.js* file from a different location into the location where Ghost expects to find it, since the ConfigMap can only mount directories, not individual files. Ghost expects other files that are not in that ConfigMap to be present in its directory, and thus we cannot simply mount the entire ConfigMap into */var/lib/ghost*.

You can run this with:

```
$ kubectl apply -f ghost.yaml
```

Once the pod is up and running, you can expose it as a service with:

```
$ kubectl expose deployments ghost --port=2368
```

Once the service is exposed, you can use the kubectl proxy command to access the Ghost server:

```
$ kubectl proxy
```

Then visit *http://localhost:8001/api/v1/namespaces/default/services/ghost/proxy/* in your web browser to begin interacting with Ghost.

Ghost + MySQL

Of course, this example isn't very scalable, or even reliable, since the contents of the blog are stored in a local file inside the container. A more scalable approach is to store the blog's data in a MySQL database.

To do this, first modify *config.js* to include:

```
...
database: {
    client: 'mysql',
    connection: {
        host     : 'mysql',
        user     : 'root',
        password : 'root',
        database : 'ghost_db',
        charset  : 'utf8'
    }
},
...
```

Next, create a new `ghost-config` ConfigMap object:

```
$ kubectl create configmap ghost-config-mysql --from-file config.js
```

Then update the Ghost deployment to change the name of the ConfigMap mounted from `config-map` to `config-map-mysql`:

```
...
    - configMap:
        name: ghost-config-mysql
...
```

Using the instructions from "Kubernetes-Native Storage with StatefulSets" on page 146, deploy a MySQL server in your Kubernetes cluster. Make sure that it has a service named `mysql` defined as well.

You will need to create the database in the MySQL database:

```
$ kubectl exec -it mysql-zzmlw -- mysql -u root -p
Enter password:
Welcome to the MySQL monitor.  Commands end with ; or \g.
...

mysql> create database ghost_db;
...
```

Finally, perform a rollout to deploy this new configuration.

```
$ kubectl apply -f ghost.yaml
```

Because your Ghost server is now decoupled from its database, you can scale up your Ghost server and it will continue to share the data across all replicas.

Edit *ghost.yaml* to set `spec.replicas` to 3, then run:

```
$ kubectl apply -f ghost.yaml
```

Your ghost installation is now scaled up to three replicas.

Redis

Redis is a popular in-memory key/value store, with numerous additional features. It's an interesting application to deploy because it is a good example of the value of the Kubernetes Pod abstraction. This is because a reliable Redis installation actually is two programs working together. The first is `redis-server`, which implements the key/value store, and the other is `redis-sentinel`, which implements health checking and failover for a replicated Redis cluster.

When Redis is deployed in a replicated manner, there is a single master server that can be used for both read and write operations. Additionally, there are other replica servers that duplicate the data written to the master and can be used for load-balancing read operations. Any of these replicas can fail over to become the master if the original master fails. This failover is performed by the Redis sentinel. In our deployment, both a Redis server and a Redis sentinel are colocated in the same file.

Configuring Redis

As before, we're going to use Kubernetes ConfigMaps to configure our Redis installation. Redis needs separate configurations for the master and slave replicas. To configure the master, create a file named *master.conf* that contains the code in Example 14-5.

Example 14-5. master.conf

```
bind 0.0.0.0
port 6379

dir /redis-data
```

This directs Redis to bind to all network interfaces on port 6379 (the default Redis port) and store its files in the */redis-data* directory.

The slave configuration is identical, but it adds a single `slaveof` directive. Create a file named *slave.conf* that contains what's in Example 14-6.

Example 14-6. slave.conf

```
bind 0.0.0.0
port 6379

dir .

slaveof redis-0.redis 6379
```

Notice that we are using `redis-0.redis` for the name of the master. We will set up this name using a service and a StatefulSet.

We also need a configuration for the Redis sentinel. Create a file named *sentinel.conf* with the contents of Example 14-7.

Example 14-7. sentinel.conf

```
bind 0.0.0.0
port 26379

sentinel monitor redis redis-0.redis 6379 2
sentinel parallel-syncs redis 1
sentinel down-after-milliseconds redis 10000
sentinel failover-timeout redis 20000
```

Now that we have all of our configuration files, we need to create a couple of simple wrapper scripts to use in our StatefulSet deployment.

The first script simply looks at the hostname for the Pod and determines whether this is the master or a slave, and launches Redis with the appropriate configuration. Create a file named *init.sh* containing the code in Example 14-8.

Example 14-8. init.sh

```
#!/bin/bash
if [[ ${HOSTNAME} == 'redis-0' ]]; then
  redis-server /redis-config/master.conf
else
  redis-server /redis-config/slave.conf
fi
```

The other script is for the sentinel. In this case it is necessary because we need to wait for the `redis-0.redis` DNS name to become available. Create a script named *sentinel.sh* containing the code in Example 14-9.

Example 14-9. sentinel.sh

```bash
#!/bin/bash
while ! ping -c 1 redis-0.redis; do
  echo 'Waiting for server'
  sleep 1
done

redis-sentinel /redis-config/sentinel.conf
```

Now we need to package all of these files up into a ConfigMap object. You can do this with a single command line:

```
$ kubectl create configmap \
  --from-file=slave.conf=./slave.conf \
  --from-file=master.conf=./master.conf \
  --from-file=sentinel.conf=./sentinel.conf \
  --from-file=init.sh=./init.sh \
  --from-file=sentinel.sh=./sentinel.sh \
  redis-config
```

Creating a Redis Service

The next step in deploying Redis is to create a Kubernetes service that will provide naming and discovery for the Redis replicas (e.g., `redis-0.redis`). To do this, we create a service without a cluster IP address (Example 14-10).

Example 14-10. redis-service.yaml

```yaml
apiVersion: v1
kind: Service
metadata:
  name: redis
spec:
  ports:
  - port: 6379
    name: peer
  clusterIP: None
  selector:
    app: redis
```

You can create this service with `kubectl apply -f redis-service.yaml`. Don't worry that the Pods for the service don't exist yet. Kubernetes doesn't care; it will add the right names when the Pods are created.

Deploying Redis

We're ready to deploy our Redis cluster. To do this we're going to use a StatefulSet. We introduced StatefulSets in "Manually Replicated MongoDB with StatefulSets" on page

147, when we discussed our MongoDB installation. StatefulSets provide indexing (e.g., `redis-0.redis`) as well as ordered creation and deletion semantics (`redis-0` will always be created before `redis-1`, and so on). They're quite useful for stateful applications like Redis, but honestly, they basically look like Kubernetes `Deployments`. For our Redis cluster, here's what the StatefulSet looks like Example 14-11.

Example 14-11. redis.yaml

```
apiVersion: apps/v1beta1
kind: StatefulSet
metadata:
  name: redis
spec:
  replicas: 3
  serviceName: redis
  template:
    metadata:
      labels:
        app: redis
    spec:
      containers:
      - command: [sh, -c, source /redis-config/init.sh ]
        image: redis:3.2.7-alpine
        name: redis
        ports:
        - containerPort: 6379
          name: redis
        volumeMounts:
        - mountPath: /redis-config
          name: config
        - mountPath: /redis-data
          name: data
      - command: [sh, -c, source /redis-config/sentinel.sh]
        image: redis:3.2.7-alpine
        name: sentinel
        volumeMounts:
        - mountPath: /redis-config
          name: config
      volumes:
      - configMap:
          defaultMode: 420
          name: redis-config
        name: config
      - emptyDir:
        name: data
```

You can see that there are two containers in this Pod. One runs the *init.sh* script that we created and the main Redis server, and the other is the sentinel that monitors the servers.

You can also note that there are two volumes defined in the Pod. One is the volume that uses our ConfigMap to configure the two Redis applications, and the other is a simple `emptyDir` volume that is mapped into the Redis server container to hold the application data so that it survives a container restart. For a more reliable Redis installation this could be a network-attached disk, as discussed in Chapter 13.

Now that we've defined our Redis cluster, we can create it using:

```
$ kubectl apply -f redis.yaml
```

Playing with Our Redis Cluster

To demonstrate that we've actually successfully created a Redis cluster, we can perform some tests.

First, we can determine which server the Redis sentinel believes is the master. To do this, we can run the `redis-cli` command in one of the pods:

```
$ kubectl exec redis-2 -c redis \
    -- redis-cli -p 26379 sentinel get-master-addr-by-name redis
```

This should print out the IP address of the `redis-0` pod. You can confirm this using `kubectl get pods -o wide`.

Next, we'll confirm that the replication is actually working.

To do this, first try to read the value `foo` from one of the replicas:

```
$ kubectl exec redis-2 -c redis -- redis-cli -p 6379 get foo
```

You should see no data in the response.

Next, try to write that data to a replica:

```
$ kubectl exec redis-2 -c redis -- redis-cli -p 6379 set foo 10
READONLY You can't write against a read only slave.
```

You can't write to a replica, because it's read-only. Let's try the same command against `redis-0`, which is the master:

```
$ kubectl exec redis-0 -c redis -- redis-cli -p 6379 set foo 10
OK
```

Now try the original read from a replica:

```
$ kubectl exec redis-2 -c redis -- redis-cli -p 6379 get foo
10
```

This shows that our cluster is set up correctly, and data is replicating between masters and slaves.

Summary

In the preceding sections we described how to deploy a variety of applications using assorted Kubernetes concepts. We saw how to put together service-based naming and discovery to deploy web frontends like Ghost as well as API servers like Parse, and we saw how Pod abstraction makes it easy to deploy the components that make up a reliable Redis cluster. Regardless of whether you will actually deploy these applications to production, the examples demonstrated patterns that you can repeat to manage your applications using Kubernetes. We hope that seeing the concepts we described in previous chapters come to life in real-world examples helps you better understand how to make Kubernetes work for you.

Building a Raspberry Pi Kubernetes Cluster

While Kubernetes is often experienced through the virtual world of public cloud computing, where the closest you get to your cluster is a web browser or a terminal, it can be a very rewarding experience to physically build a Kubernetes cluster on bare metal. Likewise, nothing compares to physically pulling the power or network on a node and watching how Kubernetes reacts to heal your application to convince you of its utility.

Building your own cluster might seem like both a challenging and an expensive effort, but fortunately it is neither. The ability to purchase low-cost, system-on-chip computer boards as well as a great deal of work by the community to make Kubernetes easier to install mean that it is possible to build a small Kubernetes cluster in a few hours.

In the following instructions, we focus on building a cluster of Raspberry Pi machines, but with slight adaptations the same instructions could be made to work with a variety of different single-board machines.

Parts List

The first thing you need to do is assemble the pieces for your cluster. In all of the examples here, we'll assume a four-node cluster. You could build a cluster of three nodes, or even a cluster of a hundred nodes if you wanted to, but four is a pretty good number.

To start, you'll need to purchase (or scrounge) the various pieces needed to build the cluster. Here is the shopping list, with some approximate prices as of the time of writing:

1. Four Raspberry Pi 3 boards (Raspberry Pi 2 will also work)—$160

2. Four SDHC memory cards, at least 8 GB (buy high-quality ones!)—$30–50

3. Four 12-inch Cat. 6 Ethernet cables—$10

4. Four 12-inch USB A–Micro USB cables—$10

5. One 5-port 10/100 Fast Ethernet switch—$10

6. One 5-port USB charger—$25

7. One Raspberry Pi stackable case capable of holding four Pis—$40 (or build your own)

8. One USB-to-barrel plug for powering the Ethernet switch (optional)—$5

The total for the cluster comes out to be about $300, which you can drop down to $200 by building a three-node cluster and skipping the case and the USB power cable for the switch (though the case and the cable really clean up the whole cluster).

One other note on memory cards: do not scrimp here. Low-end memory cards behave unpredictably and make your cluster really unstable. If you want to save some money, buy a smaller, high-quality card. High-quality 8 GB cards can be had for around $7 each online.

Anyway, once you have your parts, you're ready to move on to building the cluster.

These instructions also assume that you have a device capable of flashing an SDHC card. If you do not, you will need to purchase a USB → memory card reader/writer.

Flashing Images

The default Raspbian image now supports Docker through the standard install methods, but to make things even easier, the Hypriot project (*http://hypriot.com*) provides images with Docker preinstalled.

Visit the Hypriot downloads page (*http://blog.hypriot.com/downloads/*) and download the latest stable image. Unzip the image, and you should now have an *.img* file. The Hypriot project also provides really excellent documentation for writing this image to your memory card:

- macOS (*http://bit.ly/hypriot-docker*)
- Windows (*http://bit.ly/hypriot-windows*)
- Linux (*http://bit.ly/hypriot-linux*)

Write the same image onto each of your memory cards.

First Boot: Master

The first thing to do is to boot just your master node. Assemble your cluster, and decide which is going to be the master node. Insert the memory card, plug the board into an HDMI output, and plug a keyboard into the USB port.

Next, attach the power to boot the board.

Log in at the prompt using the username `pirate` and the password `hypriot`.

 The very first thing you should do with your Raspberry Pi (or any new device) is to change the default password. The default password for every type of install everywhere is well known by people who will misbehave given a default login to a system. This makes the internet less safe for everyone. Please change your default passwords!

Setting Up Networking

The next step is to set up networking on the master.

First, set up WiFi. This is going to be the link between your cluster and the outside world. Edit the */boot/device-init.yaml* file. Update the WiFi SSID and password to match your environment. If you ever want to switch networks, this is the file you need to edit. Once you have edited this, reboot with `sudo reboot` and validate that your networking is working.

The next step in networking is to set up a static IP address for your cluster's internal network. To do this, edit */etc/network/interfaces.d/eth0* to read:

```
allow-hotplug eth0
iface eth0 inet static
    address 10.0.0.1
    netmask 255.255.255.0
    broadcast 10.0.0.255
    gateway 10.0.0.1
```

This sets the main Ethernet interface to have the statically allocated address 10.0.0.1.

Reboot the machine to claim the 10.0.0.1 address.

Next, we're going to install DHCP on this master so it will allocate addresses to the worker nodes. Run:

```
$ apt-get install isc-dhcp-server
```

Then configure the DHCP server as follows:

```
# Set a domain name, can basically be anything
option domain-name "cluster.home";
```

```
# Use Google DNS by default, you can substitute ISP-supplied values here
option domain-name-servers 8.8.8.8, 8.8.4.4;

# We'll use 10.0.0.X for our subnet
subnet 10.0.0.0 netmask 255.255.255.0 {
    range 10.0.0.1 10.0.0.10;
    option subnet-mask 255.255.255.0;
    option broadcast-address 10.0.0.255;
    option routers 10.0.0.1;
}
default-lease-time 600;
max-lease-time 7200;
authoritative;
```

Restart the DHCP server with `sudo systemctl restart dhcpd`.

Now your machine should be handing out IP addresses. You can test this by hooking up a second machine to the switch via the Ethernet. This second machine should get the address 10.0.0.2 from the DHCP server.

Remember to edit the */boot/device-init.yaml* file to rename this machine to `node-1`.

The final step in setting up networking is setting up network address translation (NAT) so that your nodes can reach the public internet (if you want them to be able to do so).

Edit */etc/sysctl.conf* and set `net.ipv4.ip_forward=1` to turn on IP forwarding.

Then edit */etc/rc.local* (or the equivalent) and add `iptables` rules for forwarding from `eth0` to `wlan0` (and back):

```
$ iptables -t nat -A POSTROUTING -o wlan0 -j MASQUERADE
$ iptables -A FORWARD -i wlan0 -o eth0 -m state \
  --state RELATED,ESTABLISHED -j ACCEPT
$ iptables -A FORWARD -i eth0 -o wlan0 -j ACCEPT
```

At this point, basic networking setup should be complete. Plug in and power up the remaining two boards (you should see them assigned the addresses 10.0.0.3 and 10.0.0.4). Edit the */boot/device-init.yaml* file on each machine to name them `node-2` and `node-3`, respectively.

Validate this by first looking at */var/lib/dhcp/dhcpd.leases* and then SSH to the nodes (remember again to change the default password first thing). Validate that the nodes can connect to the external internet.

Extra credit

There are a couple of extra things in networking that make it easier to manage your cluster.

The first is to edit *etc/hosts* on each machine to map the names to the right addresses. On each machine, add:

```
...
10.0.0.1 kubernetes
10.0.0.2 node-1
10.0.0.3 node-2
10.0.0.4 node-3
...
```

Now you can use those names when connecting to those machines.

The second is to set up passwordless SSH access. To do this, run `ssh-keygen` and then copy the *$HOME/.ssh/id_rsa.pub* file into `/home/pirate/.ssh/authorized_keys` on node-1, node-2, and node-3.

Installing Kubernetes

At this point you should have all nodes up, with IP addresses and capable of accessing the internet. Now it's time to install Kubernetes on all of the nodes.

Using SSH, run the following commands on all nodes to the `kubelet` and `kubeadm` tools. You will need to be root for the following commands. Use `sudo su` to elevate to the root user.

First, add the encryption key for the packages:

```
# curl -s https://packages.cloud.google.com/apt/doc/apt-key.gpg | apt-key add -
```

Then add the repository to your list of repositories:

```
# echo "deb http://apt.kubernetes.io/ kubernetes-xenial main" \
    >> /etc/apt/sources.list.d/kubernetes.list
```

Finally, update and install the Kubernetes tools. This will also update all packages on your system for good measure:

```
# apt-get update
$ apt-get upgrade
$ apt-get install -y kubelet kubeadm kubectl kubernetes-cni
```

Setting Up the Cluster

On the master node (the one running DHCP and connected to the internet), run:

```
$ kubeadm init --pod-network-cidr 10.244.0.0/16 \
--api-advertise-addresses 10.0.0.1
```

Note that you are advertising your internal-facing IP address, not your external address.

Eventually, this will print out a command for joining nodes to your cluster. It will look something like:

```
$ kubeadm join --token=<token> 10.0.0.1
```

SSH onto each of the worker nodes in your cluster and run that command.

When all of that is done, you should be able to run and see your working cluster:

```
$ kubectl get nodes
```

Setting up cluster networking

You have your node-level networking setup, but you need to set up the pod-to-pod networking. Since all of the nodes in your cluster are running on the same physical Ethernet network, you can simply set up the correct routing rules in the host kernels.

The easiest way to manage this is to use the Flannel tool (*http://bit.ly/2vgBsKU*) created by CoreOS. Flannel supports a number of different routing modes; we will use the host-gw mode. You can download an example configuration from the Flannel project page (*https://github.com/coreos/flannel*):

```
$ curl https://rawgit.com/coreos/flannel/master/Documentation/kube-flannel.yml \
  > kube-flannel.yaml
```

The default configuration that CoreOS supplies uses vxlan mode instead, and also uses the AMD64 architecture instead of ARM. To fix this, open up that configuration file in your favorite editor; replace vxlan with host-gw and replace all instances of amd64 with arm.

You can also do this with the sed tool in place:

```
$ curl https://rawgit.com/coreos/flannel/master/Documentation/kube-flannel.yml \
  | sed "s/amd64/arm/g" | sed "s/vxlan/host-gw/g" \
  > kube-flannel.yaml
```

Once you have your updated *kube-flannel.yaml* file, you can create the Flannel networking setup with:

```
$ kubectl apply -f kube-flannel.yaml
```

This will create two objects, a ConfigMap used to configure Flannel and a DaemonSet that runs the actual Flannel daemon. You can inspect these with:

```
$ kubectl describe --namespace=kube-system configmaps/kube-flannel-cfg
$ kubectl describe --namespace=kube-system daemonsets/kube-flannel-ds
```

Setting up the GUI

Kubernetes ships with a rich GUI. You can install it by running:

```
$ DASHSRC=https://raw.githubusercontent.com/kubernetes/dashboard/master/
$ curl -sSL \
```

```
$DASHSRC/src/deploy/kubernetes-dashboard.yaml \
| sed "s/amd64/arm/g" \
| kubectl apply -f -
```

To access this UI, you can run `kubectl proxy` and then point your browser to *http://localhost:8001/ui*, where *localhost* is local to the master node in your cluster. To view this from your laptop/desktop, you may need to set up an SSH tunnel to the root node using `ssh -L8001:localhost:8001` *<master-ip-address>*.

Summary

At this point you should have a working Kubernetes cluster operating on your Raspberry Pis. This can be great for exploring Kubernetes. Schedule some jobs, open up the UI, and try breaking your cluster by rebooting machines or disconnecting the network.

Index

H

"headless" service, 148
Health checks example, 46-47
Heapster Pod, 84
horizontal pod autoscaling (HPA), 84-85
host filesystem, mounting, 52
Hypriot project, 168

I

immutability, value of, 3-4
imperative configuration, 4
imperative scaling of ReplicaSets, 83
installing Kubernetes, on public cloud provider, 23

J

Jobs, 95-106
    configuration, example, 97
    consumer mode, 105-106
    Job object, 95
    Job patterns, 96-106
        one shot, 96-100
        parallelism, 100-102
        work queue, 102-106
    job-oneshot-failure1-yaml, 99-100
    job-oneshot.yaml, 97
    ReplicaSet-managed work queue, 102
    restartPolicy field, 100
    service queue, 103
    work queue, 104-105

K

KaaS (Kubernetes-as-a-Service), 8
kops, for installing Kubernetes on AWS, 25
kuard application, 16, 19
    database, 19
    DNS resolver section, 67
    File system browser tab, 111
    GitHub URL, 14
    image, 18-19
    MemQ Server tab, 103
    Server Env tab, 110
    TLS key and certificate, 112
    web interface, 19, 44
kube-apiserver binary, --service-cluster-ip-range, 74
kube-proxy, 74
kube-system namespace, 29

kubeadm, 171
kubectl tool, 41, 44, 49
    checking cluster status, 26-27
    commands, 33-36
        annotate, 35-36
        apply, 35, 41, 46, 83, 98, 160-161
        autoscale rs, 85
        config set-context, 33
        cp, 36, 45
        create, 35, 80, 89, 110, 142, 147, 152, 158-106, 159, 172
        create configmap, 108, 117, 160
        create secret docker-registry, 114
        create secret generic, 112, 117-118
        creating, updating, and destroying objects, 35
        delete, 35, 40, 43, 72, 94, 102, 135
        delete deployments, 62
        delete jobs, 97, 100
        delete rs, 85
        delete rs,svc,job, 106
        describe, 34, 42, 47, 82, 116, 117, 172
        describe deployments, 125
        describe endpoints, 72
        describe jobs, 98
        describe nodes, 27-29
        describe rs, 82
        describe secrets, 113
        describe service, 70, 71
        edit, 35, 68
        edit service, 70
        exec, 36, 44, 148, 160, 165
        expose, 66, 70
        expose deployments, 159
        for debugging containers, 36
        get, 33, 40, 57-58
        get configmaps, 116
        get daemonSets, 30
        get Deployments, 122
        get endpoints, 72-73
        get hpa, 84
        get nodes, 27, 90-91, 172
        get Pods, 41
        get pods, 59, 73, 82-85, 99-100
        get replicasets, 122, 123, 127, 129
        get secrets, 116
        get services, 30, 71
        imperative scaling of ReplicaSets with, 83

About the Authors

Kelsey Hightower has worn every hat possible throughout his career in tech, and enjoys leadership roles focused on making things happen and shipping software. Kelsey is a strong open source advocate focused on building simple tools that make people smile. When he is not slinging Go code, you can catch him giving technical workshops covering everything from programming to system administration.

Joe Beda started his career at Microsoft working on Internet Explorer (he was young and naive). Throughout 7 years at Microsoft and 10 at Google, Joe has worked on GUI frameworks, real-time voice and chat, telephony, machine learning for ads, and cloud computing. Most notably, while at Google, Joe started the Google Compute Engine and, along with Brendan and Craig McLuckie, created Kubernetes. Joe is now CTO of Heptio, a startup he founded along with Craig. Joe proudly calls Seattle home.

Brendan Burns began his career with a brief stint in the software industry followed by a PhD in Robotics focused on motion planning for human-like robot arms. This was followed by a brief stint as a professor of computer science. Eventually, he returned to Seattle and joined Google, where he worked on web search infrastructure with a special focus on low-latency indexing. While at Google, he created the Kubernetes project with Joe and Craig McLuckie. Brendan is currently a Director of Engineering at Microsoft Azure.

Colophon

The animal on the cover of *Kubernetes: Up and Running* is a bottlenose dolphin (*Tursiops truncatus*).

Bottlenose dolphins live in groups typically of 10–30 members, called pods, but group size varies from single individuals to more than 1,000. Dolphins often work as a team to harvest fish schools, but they also hunt individually. Dolphins search for prey primarily using echolocation, which is similar to sonar.

The Bottlenose dolphin is found in most tropical to temperate oceans; its color is grey, with the shade of grey varying among populations; it can be bluish-grey, brownish-grey, or even nearly black, and is often darker on the back from the rostrum to behind the dorsal fin. Bottlenose dolphins have the largest brain to body mass ratio of any mammal on Earth, sharing close ratios with those of humans and other great apes, which more than likely attributes to their incredibly high intelligence and emotional intelligence.

Many of the animals on O'Reilly covers are endangered; all of them are important to the world. To learn more about how you can help, go to *animals.oreilly.com*.

The cover image is from *British Quadrapeds*. The cover fonts are URW Typewriter and Guardian Sans. The text font is Adobe Minion Pro; the heading font is Adobe Myriad Condensed; and the code font is Dalton Maag's Ubuntu Mono.

Learn from experts.
Find the answers you need.

Sign up for a **10-day free trial** to get **unlimited access** to all of the content on Safari, including Learning Paths, interactive tutorials, and curated playlists that draw from thousands of ebooks and training videos on a wide range of topics, including data, design, DevOps, management, business—and much more.

Start your free trial at:
oreilly.com/safari

(No credit card required.)

©2016 O'Reilly Media, inc. O'Reilly is a registered trademark of O'Reilly Media, Inc. D2565

Lightning Source UK Ltd.
Milton Keynes UK
UKOW05f1357031017

310329UK00002B/2/P

9 781491 935675